# The End of Anxiety

*The message that will change your life*

## Gio Zararri

Copyright © Gio Zararri

All rights reserved

ISBN: 9798646062186

*Dedicated to the person who made me understand that we can be as strong as we choose to be..*

*Thanks Mom*

| | |
|---|---|
| *Introduction* | *6* |
| *Suggestions to obtain the best benefit from this book* | *11* |
| *1 The day it all began* | *18* |
| *2 Hypochondria, your worst enemy* | *26* |
| 2.1 The importance of beginning to see the light | 34 |
| *3 The first big step: acceptance of anxiety* | *41* |
| 3.1 Symptoms of anxiety | 46 |
| 3.2 Imbalance and homeostasis | 53 |
| 3.3 A brain with a reptilian name | 58 |
| 3.4 The reason why anxiety came into your life | 64 |
| 3.5 The worries of your mind | 73 |
| 3.6 Accept and discard, your life will begin to change | 83 |
| *4 Listen to what anxiety wants to tell you* | *86* |
| *5 Smile, it is time to take action* | *93* |
| 5.1 You are the butterfly, not the caterpillar | 99 |
| 5.2 The responsibility is yours | 102 |
| 5.3 Say no to drugs | 105 |
| 5.4 There is a plant that can help you | 112 |
| 5.5 Learn to relativize, and reduce your social phobia | 115 |
| 5.6 Avoid toxic people | 120 |
| 5.7 Think positive | 125 |
| An experiment: the effect of thoughts | 129 |
| 5.8 Mens sana in corpore sano | 132 |
| 5.9 Know and recognize your best friend | 139 |
| *6 Tricks to utilize during your coexistence with anxiety* | *142* |
| *7 My life after anxiety* | *156* |
| 7.1 The benefits of anxiety | 159 |

7.2 I am and will be the strongest     167

7.3 You put the limits     175

7.4 Everything you needed has always been within you     182

*A note to the reader*     *185*

# Introduction

*If you change the way you look at the things, the things you look at change.* Wayne Dyer

*Nothing in life should be feared, it is only to be understood.* Marie Curie

*Are you looking to find a way to eliminate anxiety from your life? Do you want to feel like yourself again and not let the lack of luck control your present? Are you sick and tired of feeling those insufferable symptoms you wake up with every morning? Do you want to understand the meaning and what actions you need to take that will help you eliminate suffer and worry?*

*If at this moment your main objective is to overcome this strange problem that has appeared in your life, this book will help you.*

From my own experience I can tell you that if you stop fearing and start to understand, everything will change a lot sooner than you imagine.

This book has come to your hands with a purpose, to help you redirect your life. If you follow these simple steps, you will not only overcome your anxiety for good, but you will also be able to realize many of those dreams that you may have considered impossible.

We will try to recognize and redirect the problem for what it really is and in addition, we will fight it by trying to eliminate those frustrating sensations with the true and only purpose for which the anxiety came to your life: the need for you to make a change.

Like yourself, I had to deal with many of the symptoms you have today. I know what you are going through and I can assure you that you can overcome anxiety, you can learn from it and even stop dreading it forever.

The road that we will soon begin together is not only going to make it easier to live with the symptoms, but it will also go further. I will help you understand, that thanks to the anxiety, you will become better and stronger, overcoming the problem you have managed to overcome yourself. A complete metamorphosis.

I am not a doctor nor a psychologist, but someone close to you. A normal person who like you and many others, one day had to deal with a strange and unknown problem with the tools that he carried with him. Someone who lived the process from the inside, someone who, after many tests and more mistakes, managed to find a method that would make him overcome anxiety for the rest of his days. A path that I will soon share with you, a lesson that I hope will soon become yours.

*The End of Anxiety* is not a manual of recipes or miracles. If that is what you are looking for do not fool yourself; there are no recipes to life. To overcome anxiety is to surpass oneself, to achieve; it will depend more on your action than on your knowledge. The book that you have in your hands narrates what my process was and what my actions were and, as you will see repeated on many occasions, it will be up to you to practice what you have learned.

When you lose your way and start going against life, life sends you signals to change. At this point you have two options: Heeding and change or ignore them and follow as if nothing happened. The problem of taking the second option is that you cannot go against life forever, if you ignore their warnings for a long time life will give you a touch of attention so strong that you have no choice but to stop and... listen.

This is the message that you will make yours; the anxiety has come to your life so that you can stop and learn to listen and understand your reasoning- or not. You need a change, and this book will try to help you to understand what life wants for you.

Faced with any challenge, there are always two options: to flee or attack; to feel victimized or to take responsibility and work to overcome the problem.

If you decide to flee before facing anxiety; you can fill yourself with pills, try hypnosis sessions or psychotherapy, or just wait until the problem disappears -momentarily - but it will cost you more time and money. What is worse, is that you will live with constant fear at the idea that it can be presented again in any of its forms. If you flee, you will become dependent, and the ghost of anxiety will control your life.

Fearing anxiety leads to the reliance of anxiolytics, psychologists or external help. An enslaved life that can lead to more serious problems such as panic attacks, social phobia or agoraphobia. To sum it up, it is fear that can return without warning in any shape or form.

So, I want to help you to take the second option. The best and simplest. The most intelligent option: attack the problem by understanding the reasons why it was presented in your life and performing the actions you may need to overcome it. Understanding the reason for your symptoms, will allow you to know the motive and accept it for what it really is. It is time to act and understand that there is a before and after to your struggle, a moment that will come as soon as you decide to take control of your life.

By taking responsibility, you will take action and become a stronger and safer person; someone who directs their life and controls their fears. You will have a better understanding of what anxiety really is and what message it has to give you. This way, whether you revive or bury the damned goblin of anxiety, it will never control your life again.

When I realized that by overcoming this difficult challenge, I had become stronger and more self-confident and I had internalized new attitudes in the form of tools for life. I began to live as I really wanted to live, facing difficulties and changes of my own choosing; I understood that facing the problem made me live fearless, take control and understand that the limits are only set by you.

Once you understand changes work, the problem will begin to transform the reality around you, and you will realize that when you change the way you see things, the things you see also change.

I hope that by not being an expert on mental issues will help make your reading more enjoyable. I will try not to bore you with technicalities, complex graphics or convoluted phrases since I know from experience that this is not the best way to understand; your attention is focused on the symptoms and that is why the clearer the message, the better results.

I will try to search for a smile through these paragraphs, and from the first chapter, while turning each page. I will try to keep that smile on your face and make it stay there, as your symptoms diminish and you begin to feel better than you may have ever felt.

For any change you need action and, being this is a book of taking action, you must understand that it will not be enough to understand or accept the theory; if while the pages are moving you do not see improvements in your life, consider that you are avoiding the main objective of this book: that you take action.

Celebrate and smile because by choosing this book you have chosen to act. Soon you will understand what the message the goblin of anxiety brings to your life, you will soon discover what my steps were and what can be yours as well. You will soon feel that with each step you take you immerse yourself in that path that life really wants for you.

# Suggestions to obtain the best benefit from this book

There is a fundamental requirement to obtain the greatest benefit of both life and this book, an essential and necessary factor without it will not serve any action that you can pose.

What is the element with which you can make any dream come true?

It is one and it is quite simple: to take responsibility for our life and our happiness.

You must recognize that this change is not only possible but also necessary, from this very moment you will be able to fight and make this need a reality, considering that any strength you may need to face any difficulty situation, already exists - it was always there - within yourself.

Live this reality and perform a simple action: every time you are alone with this book, at the same time it rests in your hands, try to tell yourself: *I am responsible for my life, I can change my reality, I have the strength to make my life a better life and I know that I will soon have it.*

Also ... while you process that message that will activate the inner strength that we all carry inside, just at the moment you are going to start reading, *smile*!

Smile because you're changing, smile because you're fighting, smile because you believe in yourself again and you think you are capable, smile because you're going to take control of your own life and soon you will make something much better out of it.

This seemingly simple practice is what is making changes in you, it helps you recognize and not let you forget that you can get everything you put your mind to. Everything you consider possible you can turn it into reality.

Obtaining balance is now your most important task, you know it, and that is why you are reading these pages, for all this whenever you immerse yourself in this new reality in the form of a book, open your mouth and ... smile.

Associate this book with your change, your improvement, you will make it possible because you know it is possible. Since this is a book about taking action, associating your need for change with your new responsible self will bring you closer to your metamorphosis every day, to your improvement, while it will make it easier and more comfortable to live with the ghost of anxiety and each one of its symptoms. While you bring out that force of will that has always been in you, that force that will help you carry out the actions you need to perform.

The main goal is to overcome your anxiety, although you will realize that after this victory, you can put an end to many other fears that could have you feeling stuck. Therefore, the main objectives of this book are:

- Internalize the message that anxiety brings to your life while you accept that it has no other name.

- Carry out the necessary actions to overcome it, working on that change that life wants for you

To make the theory a reality, I try to give you some simple tips on the best way to use this book:

- Read each of the chapters as many times as you consider appropriate, if at any time there is something that you cannot understand, read it again; If you see it necessary, do what you have to do to prove to yourself that what I am telling you is true.

Do not take anything for granted, the important thing is not to read or understand, but to believe and act until the lesson learned is yours.

- Try to read in your when you are feeling calm, and if possible, read it at night before going to sleep.

Living with anxiety (especially with certain symptoms) it is very difficult to concentrate and, to solve this problem, as well as any other problem, we need to see some light in the face of so much darkness.

You need reach a state of calm but, above all, we need to believe that the goal is possible. While reading, you are already acting, you are responsible, and this book is only a tool that tries to make the way easier for you: read it, accept it, and start taking action.

Understand this manual as a gift that you are giving yourself, and that will help you improve your reality. Associate it with your moments of peace. Give yourself this option.

Have those moments close to you and immerse yourself in your way, in your life, in your needs. If you manage to recognize that you are being responsible for your problems and understand that this book can be part of your personal tools, you will be able to recover those moments of peace, necessary to make many of the actions that will restore you to balance.

- When you can, try to sleep better; believe it or not, sleep helps us to organize ideas and internalize the learning received during the day, so if you calmly get used to reading some lines before sleeping while you put them into practice during the day, before you can imagine it, you will have reached your goal.

- If you see it necessary, underline terms, paragraphs, words or phrases.

All change involves learning from mistakes and believing in your possibilities. A phrase, a word or even an image can make us light that inner strength that reminds us that we can make it possible, so if you find an idea that can help you activate this flame that is in you, record it in your memory. Use all those tools that you have available to mark with fire that new belief that makes you a stronger person.

- After internalizing and accepting your unique reality you will have to change some behaviors that make you feel out of control.

In the chapter called *Smile, the time has come to take action*, we will treat the different symptoms you suffer by carrying out the appropriate actions. We must work the change as many times as we consider necessary until all action becomes mechanical, so reread this chapter as many times as you think necessary and, above all, do not stop putting it into practice.

- As this is an action book, the best action, one that you can start doing right now and help you feel the change in a direct way is to exercise.

The best way to reduce any negative feeling is to feel its opposite, the positive, so if you can start today, I assure you that with the exercise your present will improve.

In short, to get the most from this book we should consider:

- Recognizing at all times that we are responsible for our lives. Knowing that we are fighters we will realize that we can overcome any problem that may arise. Sure of this reality and keeping this idea in our head, we will smile before these pages.

- We will associate this book with our peaceful moments, sending this association directly to our brain and, avoiding distractions that take us away from the action we are taking: working to improve ourselves.

- If possible, read before going to sleep, to help us dream, and to keep the ideas, internalize the message and mechanize the actions that will restore our balance.

- If there are phrases, words or ideas that we consider important, capable of bringing forth the inner strength that we carry within, we will underline them, take notes, or carry out the appropriate actions until they become part of ourselves.

- We will realize that we must act when the symptoms appear and we will return to the chapter of actions as many times as we need until the learning becomes an automatic response, a tool that belongs to us and that will help us overcome any difficult moment that may arise .

- If possible (and you know it is possible), we will start exercising today, assessing how our life begins to improve.

And now ... take a deep breath and smile because the time has come to begin the journey, a path that will soon make you understand that you have always been, are and will be stronger than what you have tried to believe; smile because ...

*You will be the one who will make it possible!*

*And suddenly, on any given afternoon something inside me had changed, my heartbeat was pounding with such speed and strength* that it made me understand that the end was approaching. A cold sweat ran down my temples and next to that strange and unknown beat of my heart I began to realize that I had lost control.

I still did not know that all this mess had only the beginning...

But, to recover and make that past my present, it is time to take a long journey to the inside of my thoughts....

# 1 The day it all began

*Crisis takes place when the old has not died and the new has still not been born.* Bertolt Brecht.

*I must endure the presence of a few caterpillars if I wish to become acquainted with the butterflies.* The Little Prince (Antoine de Saint-Exupery)

I was never very good at remembering names and dates, especially when I try to remember one of the most complicated moments of my life. I can relive some of the parts that followed that strange day when anxiety decided to appear in my life without warning.

I have always been quite a lazy student, for this type of person there is a day with the most depressing and harsh afternoon of the week; a day that is usually accompanied by a hangover. If you try to think about what that day might be, without a doubt, that fucking day was Sunday.

Back then I was studying Computer Engineering at the University of Deusto in Bilbao, because of this and also to an anecdote alongside a test that you will soon see, I know I was in a year between 2003 and 2006.

In the Basque Country the seasons were accompanied by colors and sensations that distinguished them, unfortunately with the climate change it is not always like that. The peculiarity of that Sunday comes to mind, a gray day accompanied by very cold temperature. With absolute certainty, it was a sad autumn Sunday.

I was living at home with my family, my parents, my little brother and my two sisters, and it was during this time, on that depressing afternoon at the beginning of the 21st century where we held a conversation about life, drugs and nonsense; a very important conversation in regards to my life with anxiety since I am sure that is what triggered it all...

I had been fooling around with drugs for a few months and this was something that worried me. That afternoon during our conversation, I realized that my foolishness was not only worrying me but it was also getting my sisters worried. I was not surprised to understand that, knowing the type of friends I had those days, they suspected and knew as much about the subject as I did, it was to be expected that they did not like the path I was taking and, in one way or another, they made me realize it.

After that talk I had no choice but to bow my head, accept that I was drifting and recognize that I needed a change. A little later I stayed at home alone, and it was during that loneliness when something inside me began to arise, something that would try to tell me that I was not only disappointing my family but also myself.

That dark loneliness that was surrounded by the odious companions: hangover and dreadful Sunday's, would soon meet a new enemy, a new unknown and serious internal problem provoked by that personal critic known as conscience.

Whilst having that conversation with my sisters, not only did I witness a strong disapproval in their eyes, but there was something else: a kind of love accompanied by fear. Their feelings, their words, and especially their glance said so much without having to say anything, had moved something inside me.

I had no idea that these factors along with others could activate the most devastating biological bomb I had ever thought could exist.

Morally, I had been feeling ashamed for weeks when I realized that I was doing something that had nothing to do with me or the life I wanted, and that the conversation I had with two of my loved ones would be the last straw, or better yet, it would be the spark that ignited the bomb, that - without having a clue – was always within me.

At the very moment when my sisters left the house and I heard the door closing, an indescribable and unknown panic has so far seized me.

Lost, confused and feeling more alone than ever, I had to fight against a swirl of thoughts and emotions so uncontrolled and excessive, I had no idea how to stop it. It was the amount of thoughts and emotions that clouded my mind at that moment that my instinctive response was very simple, I began to cry.

I cried without feeling the need to do it, in fact, the tears came only from one of my eyes; the right one. Tears accompanied by a strange nervous tic that, even without understanding why, would not cease for days.

Minutes later - still with tears in the eye - the sensation continued to worsen because to that emotional pain along with the strange tic, was another new discomfort, this time it was physical; my heart had begun to throb so aggressively that my whole body vibrated to its sound.

New and unknown symptoms were adding up, my vision began to cloud, and I started to feel a pinch in the head. Cold sweat flooded my body while great dizziness made me fear that I would soon lose my knowledge and I would fall to the ground.

I did not know the purpose for all this because neither in my reasoning nor in my memory existed a known answer, so I began to think that maybe my time had arrived...

Frightened and confused, I did my best to go to the bathroom and fought the impending faint that I soon believed would make me lose consciousness. Once I arrived, I sat down and automatically began to wet my face and neck trying to recover the control I felt was lost.

I did not know what was happening to me, but those alarming symptoms made me think and believe that everything had a name. One that I did not like, and even less, one that I hoped I could not reach my life so soon: a heart attack.

Everyone knows someone who in turn knows of people who have suffered a heart attack and, along with those symptoms accompanied by such loud, fast and thunderous heartbeats, my first conclusion would be this. I did not realize that in my fear my breath was becoming choppy and as I would later understand, the less oxygen, trapped the feeling of dizziness would increase. I ignored that the many symptoms were related to each other and by panicking, I made everything worse.

In the face of my ignorance and struggle for survival, I repeated instinctively the action of soaking myself to avoid fainting. As if repeating this simple task would endure stoically the arrival of an end that already was believed to be certain.

The seconds passed until they became minutes and, although everything seemed strange, the symptoms did not disappear and surprisingly I did not either...

Doing my best to keep myself on my feet and not knowing the time that had passed, I heard the door of my house open, voices indicating that my parents had arrived and that recognizing that I was no longer alone helped me find some peace.

Being that it were my parents who presented themselves and thinking that everything was due to circumstances that I could hardly accept, I tried to cover up my symptoms by locking myself in the bathroom and pretending I had a much more common and less disturbing stomach problem.

All the whirlwind of thoughts and emotions joined by those incomprehensible physical symptoms made it very difficult for me to devise a plan. So, I decided to continue holding myself locked in the toilet until I could discern a solution.

I understood that the best solution was to wait for one of my siblings to arrive (in those days they did not use mobile phones) to accompany me to the hospital to treat that sudden heart attack that, without understanding how, I still believed I recognized and could tolerate.

It felt like eternity until my sisters returned home, and without noticing what I felt - although the tears in my right eye made it difficult to hide - I told them that something serious was happening to me. I felt that everything was ending, I explained that I needed them to take me to the emergency room as soon as possible. A few seconds later, we were on our way.

When we arrived at the reception I explained my symptoms to the nurse on duty, and minutes later, I began to understand the reason, why so many people lamented the Spanish healthcare system.

I was infuriated to observe that, with the clear symptoms of an overdose or a heart attack, the nurse could not think of anything but to send me to the waiting room. I couldn't understand how they could make me wait while seeing such alarming physical protests. So, I made the saying of ... *how bad we were in Spain*!

Several minutes later, still somewhat pissed off by the - as I saw it - unnecessary waiting, the same nurse indicated I could get in line, that a doctor was waiting for me.

After entering the room, a doctor dressed in a white robe with a small device, known as a stethoscope, was waiting for me. Understanding that they were going to carry out such important tests with such a small object and, in my opinion, quite useless to deal with such serious problem, helped to confirm my theory about the health system.

Fortunately, I would soon see how the doctor, after a long wait of trying to treat something so serious with such a simple object, realized that the situation could be more worrisome than initially thought; after a moment's absence, she returned accompanied by a much larger apparatus suitable for treating my symptoms, an electrocardiogram.

I assumed that by detecting my heart, all jokes were aside. They decided to give me more serious tests, and this reality helped calm me down.

I was sure I had suffered something serious, I only had to wait for the results but the final diagnosis would confirm that all these surprises had done nothing more than just begin...

According to the doctor, all the inner turmoil, all those protests that seemed to keep me away from every second of life, those heartbeats that spread the palpitations of my heart to the stretcher I was in, had a name, a problem apparently quite common and had little or no danger. According to his diagnosis, I did not suffer anything serious, I had only come face-to-face for the first time with something unknown to me, a fairly common reality called anxiety.

I remembered hearing about this disorder and even knew people who were suffering from it, but considered, perhaps as a rookie in these proceedings, that what I felt was something much more serious. I was sure that there was some mistake. I felt that life had escaped me and I saw how those doctors referred to something that I considered simple, generic and apparently not as dangerous as anxiety. Personally I could not believe all of it.

The magnitude of my sensations at least helped the doctor understand my difficulties with these news. So, she prescribed some pills called anxiolytics that, would help me fall asleep and feel better.

In comprehended and sure of suffering with a much greater problem, I went back home with my sisters. I did not know that those alarming symptoms would accompany me for many more days, weeks and months. A lot longer than I would have imagined possible.

Whatever it was, something inside me was changing. If the healthcare system couldn't discover it, I will have to fight to know what my real problem was.

I was beginning to discern what would be my best medicine. I felt that I was risking my sense of survival, and therefore a courageous attitude was born within me.

*Grow in yourself a fighting attitude in the face of difficulties.*

# 2 Hypochondria, your worst enemy

*Worry does not empty tomorrow of its own sorrow, it empties today of its strengths... Corrie ten Boom*

That same day returning from the hospital, not accepting that my problem could be something as simple as anxiety, I exposed my disagreement to my sisters. I told them that in my opinion, doctors dealing with any problem, and without proper diagnosis put everything in the same category and decided to call it anxiety. I thought I was suffering from something much more serious, although to be honest, I knew very little about this disease.

I understood that anxiety was more of a mental thing than a physical one, and I felt that the doctors were evading their responsibility because I was sure that something really serious was happening to me. The symptoms were clear and quite striking, to begin with, I had never in my life seen anyone tremble at the beat of their heartbeat.

Far from helping me calm me down, that diagnosis managed to do the opposite. The way in which the doctor took away the value from my problems referring it to something generic such as anxiety, could have made me think that the true diagnosis could be much more serious. Before knowing the news for several hours, my sight had been fogged up, constant tachycardia, cold sweats and a feeling that at any moment I could lose consciousness and fall to the ground.

I also did not know that from that moment the days would cease to be days, including nights; at least in the way in which I knew them until then.

Before such symptoms, life became much more complicated. Every day that passed I became more aware of the difficulty I had in carrying out activities that I considered to be simple since, startled by the quality and quantity of my symptoms, I could not turn my attention from them. And if the symptoms were annoying for the day, I would soon realize that they would be much worse at night...

That first night after recognizing that strangely as it seemed, I was still alive and even felt sleepy as any other night. I went to bed to try to rest, hoping that those insufferable sensations also decided to take a break. I did not know that just as my body echoed the rhythm of my heartbeat, my bed would do the same. I also did not know that to the dizziness, sweating, my thoughts, shortness of breath and the rest of the symptoms I was suffering, would also like to accompany me while I was asleep.

Knowing that I was supposed to continue leading a "seemingly normal" life, and that the next day I had to go back to school, and realizing that it would be impossible to sleep, I agreed to use those pills that the doctor had prescribed.

From that day, the nights accompanied by dreams, that placidity that makes hard to wake up, that peace, or reset of your mind; everything that I associated with sleeping, had disappeared. The nights were perhaps more difficult than the days, since in the darkness I was completely alone. My nights were formed by me, my symptoms and that impotence that I began to feel when I realized that these did not disappear but on the contrary, they became stronger.

For several months I could hardly sleep, and when I did I would not even notice it. I can imagine that you know the physical and mental exhaustion that causes this.

Cold sweat, palpitations, lightheadedness, together with the trembling of my heartbeat that moved everything around me making me remember the movie of the exorcist, nightmares without sleep, constant heart attacks, cyclical thoughts that did not lead to any solution other than insanity, a maddening preoccupation preoccupied with accompanying my symptoms' loneliness, of my dreams, in this (and surely many other difficulties) had become my nights.

It all started from that stage in which one day I would decide to experiment with some drugs. I recognized that although it had not lasted a long, and it was a fairly light approach, drugs had a lot to do with that new me I had become.

A few months before, one of my friends, specifically the nerd of the group, started to use speed on the weekends. The rest of the group and I tried to understand his motives in the best way we could: by trying it as well.

Without becoming dependent or using the drug for purposes other than to flirt on the weekends, that substance became part of my free time for the last two months.

I can remember the first time I tried it, I was pleasantly surprised by its effects...

It was summer and I worked weekdays to earn some money to pay for some of my expenses. Since it was a lot of physical work, when

Friday arrived, I lacked both physical and mental energy. During those days, to amuse myself, I liked doing it.

That first hit gave me a rush of energy that I had never experienced before with anything natural, this energy made me feel not only physically stronger but above all, more mentally agile and because of the work I did in those days, energy was scarce.

In those days, my main objective on the weekend was a very simple one: to flirt; and that substance made me feel like a perfect hunter. These results made me like it, so I kept fooling around with it when the occasion presented itself. The faintness would have an expiration date, and my friends and I began to feel certain side effects that we did not like very much.

During the time that this stage lasted, several things made me realize that I was wrong. One of the worst feelings was to frequent bars or discos full of people dependent of the drug. It was so much that, the party began on a Thursday morning and finished on a Sunday night. That superficiality, that abuse of the body in such a stupid way to get in return so little together with seeing and recognizing that many people were literally hung, made me understand that all that, besides being dangerous, was not for me.

Fortunately, the harmful effects of that period in my life began to unravel. A friend had to be taken by an ambulance after experiencing a strong tachycardia. Another had a problem that was very similar to the diagnosis I was given, and that was so hard to accept.

In my case, that great change in my life called anxiety put a before and after in the game with drugs.

Understanding the latest of events from that period, I realized that drugs had a lot to do with my new symptoms and, because I did not want my parents to consider me a "jaded junky", I tried to keep it silent as best I could.

The days went by and I did not see any improvement, I felt as if my life had changed forever and it was difficult for me to talk about it with anyone. I tried to disguise the symphonic orchestra that my body had become and, helped by that fierce instinct that was born inside me when I felt the urge to discover the truth about my illness (and not the one I had been diagnosed with). I tried to face my new problem alone.

My initial requirement was to find out what my true diagnosis was since I did not accept the one I was given. Assured of the failed judgement, I began to investigate on my own, a serious mistake that would soon become a great lesson.

In those days, the internet did not work as we know it today; the information was a lot harder to find. The closest thing to Google was called a library and that is where I would spend a good amount of afternoons investigating my reality.

Anyone who knew me would think I was going crazy, not so much for my new physical features and my eyes resembling plates but because they did not understand such a radical change in my habits. I was never very diligent to the libraries, and the new me, had become one of its best customers.

I began to focus my investigations on the symptoms that worried me the most: my heart, my dizziness, and that kind of cloudy sight that accompanied me with every blink of the eye. After looking at books and more books and getting an idea of what could be happening to me, I began to appreciate two terrible possibilities: heart problems or cancer.

While researching more about the heart, I began to discover information associated with heart problems while observing and studying myself constantly to discover any symptoms that could help me recognize that serious illness I was suffering.

Days went by and every time I felt worse. I did not find any heart disease that justified the great amount and variety of symptoms that I was feeling.

I realized that the heart, while acting in a new and unknown way, did not fail, so I started to investigate the other possibility ... which got me the same results.

Days passed by and I realized that none of these diseases combined as many different symptoms as I felt. Slowly, I understood that my research did not give results and, what was worse, investigating and observing different diseases and trying to discover them inside me. I felt worse every time, this introspection without direction or meaning did nothing but worsen my true problem.

Mentally, things were not improving. Cyclical and meaningless thoughts that brought me nowhere made me realize that I might be starting to lose my mind.

Over time, this last thought was the one that terrified me the most. It was not the cancer or a possible heart disease; but the worst of my fears, was to have lost or to be losing my reasoning.

Insanity worried me because I realized that one of the direct effects of "fooling around" with drugs, one of the most well-known sequels, apart from dying from an overdose (which had not yet happened), was the stupidity and those very mysterious symptoms and such a radical change in my life, I felt anything but normal.

I have always believed that insanity is something that no one can escape, something that can occur to anyone and, in those days, I thought that something could be born inside me because I could not control my mind. I recognized that for me to be crazy was the same to be dead since not being aware of what you are living is the same as not living it.

Being my own doctor, trying to be alert and giving meaning to each of my symptoms had led to the hypochondria, increasing and the hypochondria along with my fear of insanity made me decide that I should give up in my investigations and seek other, healthier help.

Without realizing it, I had made the worst of mistakes to face my problem, a problem I would soon discover was none other than that first diagnosis that I had not wanted to accept or investigate.

Trying to combat anxiety by believing that we suffer from other diseases by focusing and exaggerating the potentiality of our symptoms is the same as trying to leave a room full of traps walking in the dark. With every step you take, you do nothing but hurt yourself more and more; the best and only solution to the problem is to find some light to discover the door that will finally allow you to escape the trap you are in.

Making the decision to seek help was not easy, but faced with the anguished fear of losing my head and recognizing the few fruits of so many blind steps, I found nothing more important at that moment than to keep alive and sane, and even with the fear that my parents came to discover some of the causes of my condition, I talked to them and told them that I needed a psychologist.

After several months accompanied by seemingly senseless suffering, without even realizing it, I had just made the best decision to overcome that problem, a decision that would make things start to change in order to start seeing some light after so much darkness.

To try to explain the importance of looking for that light that can help us solve our problems, I'll use an experience where going blind was about to cause me major headaches...

## 2.1 The importance of beginning to see the light

*Happiness can be found, even in the darkest of times, only if you remember to turn on the light. The Prisoner, by* Azkaban de J.K. Rowling.

If you overcome anxiety in the way that I am trying to help you understand in this book, you will realize how to facing this problem can allow you to become a new and better version of yourself. You will become someone much more tenacious than you thought possible. It happened to me and it will happen to you (if you want) sooner than you imagine.

Having overcome that difficult and unknown problem and feeling stronger than ever, I realized that my life needed new challenges. In those days, there was a place in the world that I wanted to see and, with the help of this new strength, I tried to create a new reality by flying towards it. A few months later, I was at the airport waiting for a plane to reach this dream. I was on my way to the eternal city; destination, Rome.

In love with the possibilities of knowing and discovering the hidden treasures in the - in my opinion – the most mysterious city in the world, I searched and found the way to make this experience come true. Once I was there, I fell in love with the city and its people that cost me more than nine years to finish a stage that initially should not have lasted more than four months.

After several years in the *Caput Mundi*, I began to observe how every two or three years an internal need to change of location was in me; whether for comfort, friends or a necessity for change, came a time of a period to move and venture to know other realities.

It was in one of these periods when a friend of mine told me about renting a room very close to the Vatican. After visiting the house and excited about the beauty of the apartment and the area, a few days later I would move to what would soon become my new home.

The day after making the move to this new apartment, my Roman friend Mattiacci convinced me (I must say it was quite easy to get it) to party. In those years I worked in the university and, if I tell you that it was normal to go out partying four days a week, maybe I am selling it short, to say the least.

I did not know the house very well, and during that party I caught a great melody. These two ingredients would make something extraordinary that night. From that hangover accompanied by the shame to remembering how the night had ended.

Many parties carry with them a great deal of memories, but that night, at least during the time that passed between arriving home and entering my bed, would not be like that. Those moments would be burned in my memory...

I remember when I reached the door of my new home I felt a terrible desire to go to the bathroom and let out those liquids that occupied my belly, because of this, I climbed the stairs as fast as I could and (always happens the same) keys in the door lock; At this point our brain makes us understand the closeness of the bathroom with which, unconsciously, we lower our guard and we can hardly retain the fluids for a long time; so, after opening the door ... I ran!

In a hurry and before the novelty of a house almost unknown to me, it was quite difficult to remember where the lights were, what I did know was that in the middle of the hall was the bathroom so quickly and in the dark I headed there.

When I finally got to what I understood was the bathroom, I opened the door and looked for the lights. As I remembered the switch had to be to the right of the door once opened, but, incomprehensibly it was not there, I did not give much importance since being a new tenant, had used that bathroom once or twice and understood that I could be wrong or remember bad location of some things.

Being a priority to release those liquids that were threatening to come out, I decided to walk by the hallway towards the bathroom, once again, in the dark.

My brain recognized what could be the distance by eyeballing so, a few steps later, I turned right, where the toilet was supposed to be, in the dark, I started looking for it with my hands.

My limbs began to move in search of the precious object where I could relieve myself, I couldn't stand it any longer, and, strangely as the toilet looked, just as it had happened with the lights, it was not where it was supposed to be.

Given the imminence of an uncontrolled escape, my head made a simple and quick observation. Common sense told me: you may have been on the wrong side. I quickly turned my body 180 degrees trying to locate once more the increasingly precious toilet.

I still found nothing, but in almost complete darkness my eyes appreciated a gleaming white object that made me understand that my body could finally discharge such a heavy load and get that long-awaited peace. The long-desired of a glowing white toilet was finally ... in front of me.

Standing with my fly down and my hands trying to steer my body towards the precious target, a voice inside me moved me to a new reality.

A few meters behind me the voice slightly transformed by my flat mate's dream repeatedly calling my name, again and again...

My logic was that I was in the bathroom so I could not understand that she could be in what I think (due to the location from which the voices came) was the bathtub. My first thought was: What the fuck is my roommate doing sleeping in the bathtub? I could not understand it, but just in case, I decided to raise the zipper by hiding my parts while trying to make some sense of it.

Within a few moments, there was light inside my head...

Ignorant of how my new house layout was, and sure that there wasn't a person in the world who could use a bathtub as a mattress, I later realized that this was not the bathroom but my flat mate's, Iona's room. I had just made one of the biggest, and simultaneously funny mistakes of my existence.

Faced with such a discovery and without fully understanding how I could have been mistaken, guided almost exclusively by that question of life and death in which this biological necessity had become, I considered the need of explaining my error as secondary, since it would not have been well seen do both at once and ... the first could not hold it for much longer.

Quickly and without saying a word, I left the room and went to the nearest one; here the light was in its place, the bathtub and even the most sought after object, the toilet, were just where I remembered they should be. Finally, I had reached the bathroom

Knowing what time it was and realizing my tremendous mistake, I found no better solution than to go to my room and to sleep it off, then the next day I would think of how to explain to my flat mate (who I barely knew) the reason for my clueless attempt to urinate in his room.

The following day, after waking up, I remembered everything and a deep feeling of embarrassment enveloped in me. It was time to apologize, and fortunately, after a pleasant conversation I understood that that precious object that I confused with the toilet was nothing else than Iona's book of legal law, a white-backed book, resplendent, as bright as a toilet seat illuminated by the moonlight.

Luckily, thanks to my mate's good sense of humor, that incident made me understand my great mistake and although it did not stop becoming a funny anecdote, I know that having pissed on his book, things would have changed a lot. I thought it might have been even worse if for any reason it had occurred to me to take a shower and it was this thought that helped me to relativize the problem by making a slight smile appear on my face.

The message that this story can bring with it could be this: before the internal need to recover peace, we need a light, a signal, an order, otherwise the brain can play us badly. We can look where we should not and end up pissing out of the cup or worse, in our partner's law book, or perhaps stepping on her belly or some nearby body part, all that would do is make the problem worse.

The same thing happens with anxiety, we need to place ourselves on the right path, find and switch on the light and figure out which is the correct "toilet", the correct path, the correct goal and what our needs are.

We should not associate what happens to us with what we can deduce by self-diagnosing ourselves, because in the same way that happened to me, we can mistake a room, and make an even more serious mistake that is far from helping us lead a better life.

Given the unknown initial problem, that decision to seek help would be the light that, slowly, would help me find the goal, to let go of what made me so bad, to unload and, to find balance, the peace that is so necessary sometimes on the road called life.

It all starts with a first step: entering the correct room, forgetting other possible diseases, and letting go of the madness to focus on and understand what anxiety really was, realizing that what he suffered could not be called otherwise.

If you are willing to see and accept reality, understand and ensure that anxiety is the issue and, you will see how the path to a solution is much easier. *With direction, your life will begin to change.*

It may also be difficult for you to accept that your real problem is summed up in something as seemingly simple as anxiety. You may think you know what your motive is, or you overlook the past or some personal problem that helps you believe that your disorder is good different; it may, and this is the most important thing, you do not know what anxiety really is and without realizing it you have not given yourself the possibility of wanting to know and understand its true meaning.

I encourage you to change your perspective. I will try to help you understand what this disorder is really about and, I am sure, you will soon discover that there are no other possibilities. I will help you to ensure that there is no other disease that encompasses as many different symptoms as you suffer today, once you begin to accept this reality you have taken a giant step towards your complete recovery.

*To resolve any conflict we need direction and clarity, turning on the light will bring us back to reality.*

# 3 The first big step: acceptance of anxiety

*A journey of a thousand miles begins with a single step.* Lao Tso

*It´s not what happens to you, but how you react to it that matters.* Epictetus

I have seen three psychologists in my life. I think it is much easier to be objective with another person than with yourself and therefore I understand that seeking help or advice outside, when you do not find it inside can be a smart and courageous solution. Being that our health is an important topic, not just any answer will help, it is necessary to find who really can, and want to help us.

Among the psychologists I have frequented, I can assure that two of them did not help me in the least.

One was trying to observe and listen to me while his gestures changed with every word that I said. He looked for the causes in my past but didn´t want to know anything of the present. Not feeling any change and understanding that not only did I waste my time but also my money, I decided to leave it.

The other one did not even explain my thoughts, he not only jotted in my childhood but went much further trying to know the childhood of my great-grandparents and great-grandparents, I believed that my internal conflicts had roots very distant, so much that, he believed they had discovered in a great-great-grandfather who more than a hundred years ago would die shot by the Francoist troops. I considered that this psychologist was much more gone than I was, so thinking about my mental health and about moving away of unknown tares, I said goodbye to him forever.

There was one who did help me, this time to a great extent. The one who knew me and encouraged me to overcome one of the most complicated stages of my youth, a person who made me see the light and take action, someone who encouraged me to get on the right path to remove that unknown disorder called anxiety. To make the reading easier I will call him *P*.

*P* was a health center psychologist, not a psychologist of 50 or more euros an hour, but someone with clear empathy; he had a fixed salary, and perhaps that was why he did not need to take more than one client. *P* went straight to the point, put himself in my place and looked for the best way to help me. If he saw that you were in a hurry, he made you understand that everything takes time but insists that we would get to work as soon as possible. Luckily, *P* did not need to bring up the past or stories of great-great-grandparents, he knew what he was up for and, he knew it very well.

If you think you need help understanding and overcoming anxiety by listening to someone who knows what they are talking about, I recommend that you seek a psychologist from a health center or a psychologist with good references, someone who really focuses on helping you without thinking of lengthening your time to increase their profits. I recommend professionals who base the therapy in your favor, there is no need to dig too much of your past, but rather try to change those little things that are unknown in relation to the problem that we are treating here; which I hope to soon help you understand.

*P* helped me overcome anxiety in the simplest and most effective way possible. Never with medications, visits to the past or shock therapies, *P* knew what I needed to know, I understood that the first and essential thing was for me to realize what was happening to me, that is, to understand what anxiety was and the symptoms that I suffered, "the suffering elf", belonged to no other group of diseases and less, terminal. *P* was a determinant to redirecting my life and to begin to feel the balance that I needed so much to overcome that painful and tormented disorder that appeared in my life.

*P* explained that I had to begin by accepting that what I was feeling only had one name to continue searching inside myself and observe what my symptoms were and when and why they happened. He also made it clear, that one of the fastest ways to insanity was to play doctor and diagnose yourself. Associating any symptom to another disease would only generate more anxiety, and everything else that all of that entails. He made me understand that the basis for ceasing to suffer was to simply accept and recognize what the real problem was, to understand that from this starting point, know and understand how to overcome it.

From this point, everything would begin to change. *P* would give me the bases to understand what anxiety was and what the reason for suffering was.

To believe his theory, he gave me a book that, made me focus so much on reading, that I even forgot the title. A book that left no room for doubts, a text that certified that my symptoms were not anything other than the first diagnosis I had a difficulty accepting.

My new companion in the form of a book, my symptoms, and I would give shape to the best therapy, to help me understand that everything I suffered was not something terminal and on the other hand, had a cure.

After accepting it and feeling a lot more motivated, I would get deep into the health related wording, to soon discover information that would flood my path with light: a list that showed each and every one of the symptoms of anxiety. Realizing that there was no other ailment that encompassed these physical and annoying protests, I accepted anxiety by understanding what was my real and only problem. *From that point on, everything started to change...*

Knowing that your problem has a name, defining it and knowing that it is not something terminal, makes your concern and your symptoms become relativized and diminish immediately. The basis to stop suffering unnecessarily is to recognize what your problem is, to make sure that you will not lose your head, and much less end your life, among this point, to recover peace and power and to be able *to take action.*

If you want to start feeling better, do the same. I will try to point out a list of the symptoms of anxiety so that you can observe of the many you are sure to have.

From here, you must understand that it is impossible that a disease which encompasses so many different appearances can exist.

This reality should be enough to rule out other possibilities and eliminate hypochondria, one of the worst enemies towards your recovery. Here's your first big step.

Help yourself and understand that what you are suffering has a name and, above all, cheer up and acknowledge that this does not lead to death. There is a cure, an exit that you will soon make your own. It is not the end of the world, but the beginning of a new stage which can make you a much stronger person.

This book tries to help you understand this theory, a theory that I can assure you is true, for me as for you or any other person. To recognize this reality is the first step that will lead you to peace. Slowly, you will see how the anxiety, already defined in your interior and your actions will bring with it many and very good benefits.

Eliminating death and insanity from any of the possibilities, made me gain some peace. The knowledge that $P$ and that book gave me, were indicating which way to go.

## 3.1 Symptoms of anxiety

In that book, which became my guide, many of the symptoms of anxiety were summarized, these were divided more or less like this:

- Physical symptoms: Tachycardia, palpitations, chest tightness, shortness of breath, tremors, sweating, digestive discomfort, nausea, vomiting, "knot" in the stomach, eating disorders, muscle tension and stiffness, tiredness, tingling sensation, dizziness and instability. If neurophysiological activation is too high, sleep deprivation, and sexual response may occur.

- Psychological symptoms: Restlessness, stress, sense of threat or danger, desire to flee or attack, insecurity, feeling of emptiness, strangeness or depersonalization, fear of losing control, mistrust, suspicion, uncertainty, difficulty making decisions. In more extreme cases, fear of death, insanity, or fear of suicide.

- Symptoms of behavior: alertness and hypervigilance, blockages, clumsiness or difficulty to take action, impulsivity, motor restlessness, and difficulty staying still. These symptoms are accompanied by changes in expressiveness and body language: closed postures, rigidity, awkward movements of hands and arms, jaw tension, changes in the voice, facial expression of astonishment, doubt or tension,                                                                 alertness.

- Intellectual or cognitive: Difficulties of attention, concentration and memory, increased lack of attention and neglect, excessive worry, negative expectations, rumination, distorted and inopportune thoughts, increased doubts and confusion, tendency to remember unpleasant things , overestimate small unfavorable details, abuse of prevention and suspicion, inadequate interpretations, susceptibility ...

- Social: Irritability, self-absorption, difficulties to start or continue in a conversation, in some cases, and verbiage in others, blocking or blank when asking or answering, difficulties expressing one's own opinions or asserting one's own rights , excessive fear of possible conflicts, etc.

In that manual, they explained that not all people have the same symptoms nor the same intensity, every human being is a world apart.

At this point, I would like you to observe one thing:

*How many of these symptoms are you experiencing?*

Surely more than one.

Now comes an even more important question that I hope you respond with a yes: *Can you accept that you only suffer anxiety and eliminate other possibilities? Can you accept that there is no other different disease that encompasses so many different symptoms?*

If you answered "No" to this last question, I recommend that you return to the beginning of the chapter and at the same time observe what your symptoms are. If you do not have them, try to find any other disease that includes each and every one of your symptoms, I am sure that no matter how much you investigate you will never find it.

Before you continue reading, it is very important that you have understood this first lesson: *you do not suffer anything other than anxiety.* It is important that you internalize this truth to follow the path that we are taking together, if you believe or want to continue to believe that your problem is something else, no action you decide to take will lead you back to peace.

Each person, according to their biological and / or psychological predisposition, is more vulnerable or susceptible to some or other symptoms. What was not said in the book but what the psychologist helped me understand, is that there was no mortal disease whatsoever grouping so many different symptoms; the only disease that could take such varied symptoms was the one I was facing, anxiety itself. I did not suffer anything mortal or was I going crazy since this same disorder contemplated a great number of psychological protests as could be to adopt the belief of approaching insanity.

The moment I accepted this reality, I focused on the road I had to travel and I stopped dissipating my energy on tasks or research without meaning; as soon as you do the same, your life will begin to change.

Identifying this great truth made me recuperate my joy and excitement, I continued my path to that light, that end of the tunnel that would bring me back to life.

I realized, even if I had to accept it, that both P and the doctors who performed that first diagnosis were right. Observing this new reality, I tried to recognize my symptoms and guiding myself from the previous list I underlined the ones that I suffered Being left with a list that looked something like this:

- Physical: Tachycardia, shivers, chest tightness, shortness of breath, tremors, sweating, muscle tension and stiffness, tiredness, tingling, dizziness and instability. Sleep disturbances, and certainly, although I do not remember well, alteration of the sexual response.

- Psychological: Restlessness, feeling overwhelmed, feeling of threat or danger, desire to flee or attack, insecurity, feeling of emptiness, feeling of strangeness, fear of losing control, uncertainty. In more extreme cases like mine, fear of going crazy and / or death.

- Behavior: alertness and hypervigilance, blockages, clumsiness or difficulty acting, impulsivity (especially when eating), motor restlessness, difficulty staying still and at ease.

-Intellectual or cognitive: Difficulties in attention, concentration and increase of misunderstandings and oversights, excessive worry, negative expectations, rumination (cyclical thoughts), distorted and inopportune thoughts, increased doubts and confusion, a tendency to remember above all unpleasant things, overestimating unfavorable details, abuse of prevention and suspicion, inadequate interpretations, susceptibility.

- Social: Irritability, self-absorption, difficulty initiating or following a conversation, freeze or staying blank when asking or responding (this was mainly due to having another major concern on my mind, controlling my symptoms).

Many were my own symptoms, and mostly all on the list, and next to them I felt like I was becoming a complete disaster, so much that a past experience came to mind.

As I explained at the beginning of this book, those years in which I lived with anxiety, I studied Computer Engineering and among the many subjects there was one called *Compilers* that seemed too complicated. I did not like it at all and I did not understand what its practical usefulness could be. My opinion did not matter since I had to attain the degree, I had to pass it.

After failing it in three tries, I began to feel the vital need to get rid of it once and for all. Aware that in those days (largely due to my anxiety problem) I did not socialize too much, I focused among other things on doing well on that test and eliminate this other the baggage I was dragging.

With this priority as a new goal, I spent several days studying with a friend from the university. Being an exercise-intensive exam, my friend used a technique to save paper by doing different exercises on a single sheet, his resources were based on using pencil and an eraser that, after performing an exercise and getting the answer, erase it and use the same sheet for a new one.

Since I often lacked substance, I often thought about the need to learn to be more ethical. So, I thought that technique could make sense and I used that method until that activity became second nature for me as well.

After studying thoroughly and performing a lot of exercises I felt prepared, so I was quite confident the day of the exam. I would go take it, along with my pencil and eraser, the sheets, this time, the teacher would put them.

I left the exam room quite happy, and to ensure the smile on my face, I consulted the results with some of my classmates who met at the exit; most of the answers matched so I was so glad to get that off my back.

To my surprise, days later while checking the answers on the test board, my final result was one out of ten. I had failed it again, but this time I could not believe in the fairness of that miserable grade, aware and certain that there was some mistake. I prepared to challenge the exercise and asked the professor to review the test.

Days later, I would go to the evaluation, sure to fight an injustice but, once I checked my examination I could do nothing other than to be without words. I would never have imagined seeing what my eyes saw and even less that the author would have been me...

The answer sheets of my examination were nothing but a myriad of numbers, formulas, results and meaningless scribbles, everything was ... *completely blurry*!

Blurred because I myself had erased all the answers using my saving paper technique to perform different exercises one over another.

Embarrassed, I understood that the teacher was not to blame and that there was nowhere to cut off, so I appreciated the imagination of the teacher for having given me such generous score for having that set of senseless blots. I apologized and explained that my technique linked to my concern, played a bad joke on me.

I was going to study the hell out of that subject again, but one thing was sure, next time ... *I'd use a pen*!

That was an example among so many others, which indicated to me that my excessive worry, the excessive over-thinking and observing those sensations that invaded me, did nothing but move away from life and the present, I had to attack my symptoms, I needed to come back to life .

After realizing that what I suffered had a name, to recognize that anxiety encompassed each and every one of my symptoms (including the belief that I was going crazy), I realized that I had just entered the right path to gain back control of my life .

In order to regain the balance I longed for, the only possible solution was to continue investigating (this time following the advice of P), what were the causes of that disease. Every time it became clearer, I would know a new word unknown until the moment that would make more sense to the reality of those days.

*Embark on the right path, do not try to become a doctor by creating possibilities that do not exist.*

## 3.2 Imbalance and homeostasis

*You have to look for a good balance in the movement and not in the stillness.* Bruce Lee

**Power without control is useless** Advertising slogan for the Pirelli brand

Soon I would begin to discover that anxiety or rather my desire to leave it behind, would bring new and useful knowledge to life.

I would discover that thanks to this problem I would learn more about myself, learn how to choose what went into my body and what was around me, while using tools and techniques to maintain control. I would also learn new words that would accompany me along the way, one of the ones that caught my attention the most was homeostasis, which means:

*Set of phenomena of self-regulation, leading to the maintenance of a relative constancy in the composition and properties of the internal environment of an organism...*

The pages of that book and the quotes helped to better understand my condition at that time, I was basically in a state of imbalance.

In that passage, a graph indicated the optimal level of homeostasis, the perfect equilibrium range for the correct functioning of a human being.

It also explained how our body uses internal regulation mechanisms to keep us within this balance and how, given internal factors such as stress, anxiety, diseases such as depression, or external agents such as drugs or phobias, that balance, could be broken.

It was stressed that with such imbalances (higher or lower levels of the optimal range of homeostasis) the human body stopped working normally, and therefore, the engine began to fail.

Among the effects that this disharmony caused, it could have been that the heart can pump more than usual, that excessive sweating is generated or that the iris dilates making possible the entrance of a greater amount of light. These were just some of the effects that were caused by a chemical imbalance that produced an alteration in our levels of homeostasis.

I did not need to study medicine to understand that one plus one equaled two. Things were making sense...

After many erroneous investigations trying to discover the problem that affected me, thinking about the possibility of suffering some type of cancer or coronary disease, that book, that the psychologist and this new word, made me understand that the origin of my particular history was something more basic, logical and even biological.

My body- for different reasons, many of which I had yet to discover- had become unbalanced and this was the reason why I was functioning so badly. There was nothing mystical, supernatural or mortal at all.

It only remained to discover the reasons why a body can react negatively because sincerely, I did not understand why mine behaved so badly.

My head, theoretically (leaving aside some fragments of my life as the experience with that examination that I ended up erasing) was fine, but I did not understand the need to have to sweat so much, to look so bad, to constantly hear the beating of my heart or live with that constant sensation of vertigo and dizziness.

As an ex-anxious person now I can tell you that the secret to overcoming anxiety is to follow a simple path, start by naming it and eliminating other possibilities to continue to observe and to know what your reasons are. Knowing the effects, you will come to the causes and for this, you will have to face them until you observe how they slowly disappear from your life. Facing your problems will make your causes disappear, and without causes there will be no effects, so your symptoms may disappear forever.

Think of your body as a car, if the engine fails it is useless that you try to drive it, or cursing it out, there are two options: go to the mechanic or patiently investigate the problem to find out a solution.

Although with anxiety you can feel a lot more fucked up than a mechanical failure, understanding the causes and remedying them is much easier than getting to study mechanics without having any idea of it. It can, if you need it, help you with a psychologist, but personally, seeing things the way I see them today I think it is not always necessary, if in those days a book like this would have reached my hands, I could have overcome that problem investing much less time, energy and bad times. This is why I decided to write this book, to try to help other people who, like me, back in the day, do not see an exit or understand their situation, helping them to understand that there is a way to overcome anxiety forever.

Like many people, I lived the process. I suffered what you might be suffering and surely those days were the most difficult days of my life.

I can also say that thanks to overcoming this problem, I became stronger. Today marks many years that I have lived alone, thousands of miles from home, without being conditioned by fear of the return of longing or a possible outbreak.

In my life, I have suffered many episodes of anxiety, but after understanding what I am trying to help you understand in this book, is that I've always known that I am and will be stronger than anxiety.

If you comprehend, agree, and recognize that there is nothing strange or metaphysical in this problem, if you stop associating your state with a possible mental error or defect and you eliminate the weak description for having suffered or being suffering this imbalance, if you understand which is something totally natural and you observe what the causes are, you will come to understand that there is nothing to fear but a lot to learn.

After knowing the homeostasis, you also discover that you only need to re-stabilize your body. Soon you will understand that you are, were and will always be stronger than you have sometimes believed. Anxiety will not control your life.

Discovering, accepting and limiting my reality, I felt that it was time to move to that action that would restore my balance. I needed to recover those correct levels of homeostasis that would restore my life, but before I started with that, I had to understand why it had happened to me, what were my mistakes, my causes.

Looking in my interior, I would soon find out who was responsible. The one that would unleash the emotional bomb that was inside, a brain unknown and of peculiar name was the cause of everything...

*Anxiety is the result of an internal imbalance, an alteration in our correct levels of homeostasis.*

## 3.3 A brain with a reptilian name

*What is essential is invisible to the eye.* Antoine de Saint-Exupery – The Little Prince.

*The heart has its reason of which reason knows nothing.* Blaise Pascal

My body was still acting strange. I found it hard to sleep and my life was still far from returning to what I considered a normal life, before experiencing with anxiety. I was aware of everything, but I also felt like I was making great strides towards change by recognizing that what happened to me had a name and scientific basis, and that my life was no longer in danger. All this was able to comfort me and to see that difficult present in a more positive way. My symptoms had been greatly reduced and were less likely to return. Still living with anxiety, I noticed that things began to change.

I could rule out that it was cancer or the imminent heart attack and even eliminate my biggest worry, *I was not going crazy*!

This first step brought back some peace of mind, but I still had no idea what to do to eliminate anxiety completely from my life.

To better cope with this problem, P explained to me some other trick that could help me control my so feared symptoms. Some of these can be seen in chapter six of this book. Accepting anxiety, accepting my reality and using these tricks, would not be enough to regain my balance, so I continued to investigate and tether the rope ... I would soon know why my body did not function properly, or what caused the instability in which had become of my body.

There was very interesting information that talked about the functioning of the human brain in which explained how our brain can be divided into 3 smaller ones, each of which manages different functions, and among them there was one, the smallest and oldest, which seemed to be behind the commotion in which I was sunk: *the reptilian brain.*

In a broader outline the three small brains that make up our brain are:

- The cortex or rational brain, which manages reason and logic.

- The limbic brain, which manages emotions and gives meaning to things.

- And the most internal, smallest, and surely unknown of all, the reptilian brain, which regulates the basic functions of the organism. Its main objective is *our survival.*

The book gave some clues about the influence of the reptilian brain on disorders such as anxiety, so I focused my research on it, and the more I found out about this brain, the more I realized how important it was in many aspects of our lives.

The action of research encouraged me and made me feel stronger. Making sense of something so seemingly, and meaningless as anxiety and its symptoms, made me see some light in the face of so much darkness, and that is why, learning about the reptile brain, brought a smile to my face, realizing that from here, everything made sense .

The name "reptilian" came about because it was the first brain that nature gave us, starting with the reptiles more than 500 million years ago.

The human being evolved, and with his development changed our brain and then appeared reason (cortex), and emotions (limbic system) and, in that mass of things, came our present brain. Everything was united.

As I said, the reptilian brain manages our survival by controlling basic functions of the organism, including:

- Blood flow

- Heartbeat

- Body temperature through sweat mechanisms

- The subconscious

- Digestion

- Balance

- Eye sight

- And ... many other functions of the human body.

I wanted to expose some of the functions that this brain manages with a single purpose. Maybe while you read the list you have realized why or maybe not, but if you have not noticed anything strange I encourage you to reread the list slowly and make use of your recent memory.

*Have you noticed something that has caught your attention?*

If your answer was no, there's certainly something that doesn't allow you to observe the present well, your anxiety, so I'll try to help you...

Quickly review the symptoms of anxiety and then re-read the list above (functions that regulates the reptilian brain). Did you realize that there is a direct relationship between the two lists?

This relationship is due to a fairly basic reason: it all started here! The reptilian brain was the one that gave the order to activate and give life to the anxiety in our organism.

During that time of doing my research, the light became much brighter; nightmares, heartbeat, sweating, sight and motor functions, among other symptoms, made it clearer. *It had all started here! Everything made sense!*

It was time to understand why without apparent reason, I had to continue living with such unpleasant symptoms, to understand why this old brain had felt the need to activate a response as disturbing as the anxiety in my body.

I am the type of person who thought that almost everything in this life had a reason and that, perhaps the best way to attack any type of problem is to know the source or causes that generated it. So, I came to point of the investigation and I had no intention in stopping until I understood everything.

A hemorrhoid, a cold, an allergy, that they cheat on you, and even what some like to call bad luck, usually have a cause, something that provokes everything. In this case, the imbalance generated by the reptilian brain was the effect of different causes or motives that I would soon discover.

My basic reasoning was this:

Cause-effect: One or more causes caused an imbalance activated by my reptilian brain. This brain understood the need to act causing changes in various functions of the organism, which resulted in an imbalance of the levels of homeostasis. That is how the anxiety came into my life and most likely, yours also.

I realized that in order to regain harmony, it would not be enough to rationally acknowledge that I was well and that there was no need to continue to feel all that. Something more internal to me, that primitive brain, I had to understand that it was really like this, I needed to show him that I had changed. It was time to realize that, without a doubt, something inside me was asking for a change.

At that time I believed that the cause of all my worries had been those days of "flirting with drugs". I thought that had unleashed everything but soon discovered that this was just one of the causes, there were many others that, to recover again, I had to start treating and improving. I did not know that it would be the same anxiety that would indicate the way forward...

For weeks, maybe months, I had begun to notice how my body forced me to put aside certain substances like coffee and some other kinds of food.

Just like my body, my brain also needed more peace and, unconsciously, I was taking action to get it. I stayed with the people who made me feel better and less with the ones that made me anxious. I used to go to quieter places, I exercised more, and even learned how to breathe better.

Without realizing how the anxiety affected my life, the need to feel alive again, something inside me was changing; before I knew it, I was changing too.

I have always been passionate about books of suspense, that logic with which detectives, police or different actors solved crimes or inequalities made me give a sense to the use of intelligence; to recognize the intrigue and to discover the mystery before it was revealed, made me give reason sense. Faced with anxiety, I enjoyed the same way trying to solve a case, a mystery that had come and had a direct effect on my quality of life.

Aided by my passion for intrigue, I realized that I was clarifying the enigma and this made me happy. In those times, I felt happily anxious. Recognizing these small achievements, realizing that I was improving and struggling to recover, made me endure those symptoms a lot better, but I still did not understand why, they wanted to stay.

## 3.4 The reason why anxiety came into your life

Along with my new discoveries, I recognized that I was starting the path that would help me get out of the problem, and although I still had to deal with many of my symptoms, accepting this fact and understanding that I was becoming responsible for their reality was enough for me to live with anxiety in another way.

I understood and began to enjoy the phrase "there is a bright side to everything", understanding that better things were to come. I did not focus on my symptoms but looked beyond, beginning to discover many of the benefits that, to understand and overcome this problem, could bring into my life.

The driving force that will help you to succeed is this: recognize each of your steps, understand the need for change, valuing what anxiety wants to tell you, and, above all, feel the strength of your metamorphosis, while enjoying the path and knowledge that this new stage brings to your life.

Life is a continuous learning process, and one of its great lessons speaks of the way in which we can observe a cup. If you strive to see it half full, you will, but if you do the opposite, you will be able to empty it.

Being smart and observing the benefits you can get will help you get closer to them, otherwise you will continue to blame existence until you realize that life will not change if you do not change, the sooner you understand it the sooner you will work on it and improve things first.

Following my new approach, I found it interesting to see how this brain unknown to me worked. Its main mission is to keep us alive, so to survive, manages our vital functions allowing us to react to possible threats. Its answer does not help the other two auxiliary brains, it does not ask our logic because it has its own, and when its indicators give a warning,  the reptilian brain, without needing to think twice, reacts and,  oh *how it reacts*!

To understand the logic with which it works, we must go back in time millions of years ago...

We know that human beings have lived hundreds of millions of years on earth and that the evolution of man like that of any other living being, is gradual. We can thus understand, that in terms of biological evolution, things take time. The problem is that there have been many dramatic changes in the history of mankind that some organs have not been able to evolve at the same speed.

If giraffes' necks have been growing millimeter by millimeter, every hundred years, we can understand that the same progression in time would need evolution, the same goes for the human being, but it has not always been that way...

The reality of man is quite different, since our environment has evolved more in the last hundred years than in the thirty-five million that we are on earth; taking this into account, we can understand that life as such has developed in a much more rapid way than our organism; and understanding it is easy to recognize why today, the reptilian brain is not able to distinguish between the attack of a hungry lion or, to give a current example, the loss of a job. This brain before a change that understands how dangerous it is, reacts as anxiety.

The sense of danger that may have been caused by the attack of a tiger or a rhinoceros can now be propitiated by such simple and less dangerous things - at least for our physical integrity - as a change of environment, of work, of dismissal, or the loss of a loved one, because of this, change, is the main reason why anxiety arises and is born in people.

The reptilian brain is so ancient that under certain circumstances it continues to reason in the same way as it did millions of years ago, although today's circumstances are completely different.

It is a reality in our present that, due to causes that have nothing to do with our true survival, our brain reacts as if it were and, when feeling in danger acts by triggering in its response disorders as common as: anxiety, stress or depression, the so-called diseases of the 21st century.

We have to learn to value things for what they really are and thus, from reason, not send wrong information to elements as primitive as the reptilian brain. If we use the phrase of the *Little Prince*, the essential is invisible to the eyes, it may be that realities such as anxiety present much more solid foundations and with sense of what we imagine, it may even be ourselves who, without realizing it, send indicators of danger to our reptile brain inviting him to give us a strong touch of attention. If we drill our mind with imminent dangers, our organism, whether we like it or not, reacts.

The reptilian brain understands only two ways of acting: to attack or to flee. If we understand that the danger of this brain is more associated (due to its evolution) to the attack of a tiger than to a change of work, we can understand that its most common reaction is:

- Increase the heart rate by pumping more blood to the heart to have more energy before the possibility of response, either in attack or in defense.

- Breathing becomes faster and choppy, oxygenating the muscles and giving us the possibility to run, for example.

- Muscles contract, preparing us for action.

- Our iris' dilates so that, by entering more light, we can see better and observe different possibilities or places of escape.

- Excessive and constant sweating in order to maintain internal temperature in the event that circumstances require it.

- And many other more actions, such as shitting on yourself.

All of these reactions have a single mission: to survive a physical danger, but if this danger does not exist, a crisis of panic is born which, if it is not understood and accepted for what it is, is very easy to derive in an anxiety syndrome and stay for a long period of time.

With examples like these, everything was clear; my prehistoric brain had provoked these and other changes in my body, and my reason for not understanding the change when it arose did nothing but maintain that state of alertness, the anxiety and all of its symptoms.

Somehow my primitive brain had reached indicators that made it feel that my life was in danger and it had acted the only way it knew how: by pulling the alarm and modifying my vital functions to prepare for only two possibilities it understood, to attack or flee.

Even if I did not identify or acknowledge that my life was in danger, my reptilian brain had understood otherwise. So, the (among other things) symptoms did not disappear. I had not considered until then the need for anxiety to come to me life and would like to continue in it.

Knowing the way our body acts, knowing that it is independent of the cortex (reason) and being very aware that my reason had not noticed the need (although it had probably sent many signals to the reptilian brain), I had just understood that it was impossible to eliminate my symptoms and return to the much sought after balance if I made exclusive use of logic. To this brain little cared what I thought or to assure that it would never do certain things again, this millennial organ needed to feel it, it was not enough to think necessary to act, the change had to be real and lasting.

Understanding the motives and reasons for that alarm that had come off to my reptilian intelligence and treating each of them would be the solution. Avoiding did not help; indeed, not only would I not eliminate those insufferable symptoms but, if I did so without facing this message, anxiety or fear that I might return, could determine much of the rest of my life

I considered that avoiding anxiety would condition my future, so the possible answer was not to flee but to fight. Only a change with that intensity would restore my balance to enjoy a full life without (conditioning) symptoms.

It was time to direct my actions to put an end to this duel, I was thinking, *what is needed to win this war? And what did it take to fight and win?*

The answer was obvious, to win fighting, weapons were needed, but what weapons would help me to overcome that danger that my reptilian brain observed in my life? How could he be able to fight for a better, healthier and better life? The only tools that make it possible to overcome any kind of mourning, our own abilities.

This is what the rest of the journey was about, to recover values and aptitudes that always existed within ourselves.

For one or many reasons in our life we move away from the path, our true essence, leading a life that may have very little or nothing to do with what we should follow and anxiety came into your life to make you change that course. My symptoms would indicate the changes to be made to bring to light those tools that would help me win the battle, gaining in safety and being responsible for my reality, recover the longed for balance, this would be the message that would change my life forever. ..

This time it was not enough by just believing, I needed to prove it to myself. I knew there were such impetuous elements in nature against which the exclusive use of reason had no effect. Several years ago I lived a clear example of this.

During my time in Rome, just like any other night, it was time to go to sleep, it seemed like a totally normal night but that was going to be very different from any other known to date...

In the middle of my dreams something awakened me, an unknown force began to push my bed to either side of the room I was in, the strength was so huge that it was not enough to shake me, it also did everything I surrounded. At such a paranormal event, I rubbed my eyes several times until I realized that it was not a strange dream and, moved by that strange feeling difficult to describe, I opened my eyes...

Reason told me that some of my roommates could be behind everything but, looking in all directions I realized that there was no one there, was ... completely alone!

It was a rather bizarre reality, my bed and I were moving from one place to another without any visible or known force, responsible for all that. Logic then used my memories by presenting me with a sequence of images, fragments of a film I saw years ago, The Exorcist.

Incredibly scared, I jumped out of my mattress escaping from my room, I did not know that the reality outside of my stay was going to be even more extraordinary...

In the corridor to which I opened the door, I found the rest of the roommates, something strange at that time, although the strange thing was not that they were there but the position adopted by each one of them. As it happened to me these had also left their dormitories and they were next to me, in a position similar to that of a surfer riding a great wave, but, in this unusual scene the table was the corridor and those waves and its movement, the entire floor in which we were...

Quickly, in an impulsive way, I would also start surfing, until, even though I understood nothing of what was happening, one of my companions lit the bulb and uttered a phrase. Aware of the movement and of our possible end shouted: U Tramouttttt!

When I heard that I was stoned and associating, the first thing that came to mind was the wind of Tramontana, this gave me some peace although I could not understand how in Italy there could be such strong winds capable of moving a whole house but, On second thought, if everything was due to a wind I understood that my life was not in danger.

Seconds later everything returned to calm and talking with my friend told me that the phrase I had heard was not "U tramout" but "U terremout", earthquake spoken in accent Pugliese (from the Italian region of Puglia).

It took me several minutes to realize that I had just had my first experience of an earthquake, one of the strongest and deadliest in Italy, that huge movement devastated the Aquila area, it was so strong that it literally made it sway and stagger buildings, including mine, more than 150 km from its epicenter, in the city of Rome.

Before the earthquake my colleagues and I adopted different answers, while some decided to wait at home to pass, others (among whom I was) we preferred to go out and move to a safer place, hoping that no reply would take place. I did not understand earthquakes but my friends did, and they told me that normally the strongest earthquake occurs after a first call of attention.

Fearful that the building might collapse a colleague and I decided to get out of the house and approach a nearby park. At dawn, after a walk of little more than half an hour, seeing that nothing happened, we returned home, it seemed that everything had happened and fortunately it was.

Given certain forces of nature the possibilities are always the same, to attack or to flee; sometimes our survival depends on our ability to respond. Fortunately that time was not necessary but in Aquila many people were saved thanks to their ability to react.

This example helps me understand that anxiety, an internal earthquake generated by our reptilian brain, also needs an answer, ours. It is very likely that over time other replicas will be given and, in order to be prepared, we must understand the message that brings anxiety and act accordingly.

After understanding the details of the reptilian brain and the reasons why the anxiety came to my life, I was aware of the steps to be taken and, among all of them, I had to eliminate the excessive worry that clouded everything to orient my thoughts towards its solution, not the problem.

*Anxiety comes to our lives looking for a change, ours.*

## 3.5 The worries of your mind

*Before worrying, get busy* Miguel Viejo

*My life has been full of terrible misfortunes, most of which never happened* Michel de Montaigne

The secret to rule out cancer or any terminal illness other than anxiety, was discovered when I realized that my symptoms were directly proportional to the concerns I felt.

The reptilian brain, due to known situations and others that I had yet to discover, had unleashed all this internal jumble that gave name to this book. What I did not understand until I began to notice was the importance of the way I focused on the symptoms.

The more value I gave to anxiety and what it made me feel, the stronger it was feeling. The more worried and afraid I was, the stronger the symptoms.

This helped me understand that my problem was not due to anything other than diagnosed. My life was not in danger because what physical illness increases directly to worry? Without a doubt I could say that there was none.

Understanding and accepting anxiety while understanding that your life is not in danger will eliminate your hypochondria, perhaps the best ally of anxiety, the worst enemy to regain your balance.

Accepting the anxiety I had discovered, and how the symptoms were directly proportional to my concerns, the more I focused on how the symptoms made me feel, the bigger they became.

All of this made me consider a change of mindset. I understood that if the anxiety was not going to kill me because it would not cause an imminent heart attack and it was difficult to fall to the ground due to the result of a dizziness, *why give should I give it so much worth? Why bother and let it control my life? What good was it to focus on symptoms that would not kill me?*

The reality was simpler, worrying about anxiety symptoms was not going to do me any good.

Aware of this, I began to try to coexist in a different ways with the situation. When anxiety manifested itself, it associated those sensations with different situations that could provoke it, without considering the existence as something of concern, it was learning how to relativize.

We have seen that some of the symptoms that accompany anxiety are feelings of choking, suffocation, palpitations, sweating, muscle tension, dry mouth, mental blockages, feeling of unreality, confusion, sleep problems, invaded by apathy and we even want to cry, our head becomes a washing machine centrifuging thoughts without order or meaning, reflections are repeated, crowded, questioned, prevented, threatened, made to feel that you are a waste and that you are not able to regain control of your life, in short, we are invaded by concern and this concern does not let us live.

It is time to breathe, take a moment of peace, and find a way to beat anxiety.

We must regain control. In the tricks section of the book, I will explain some of the tricks I used to eliminate or reduce the anxiety concern that filled my life. Believe it or not, you can choose the thoughts and emotions that will turn you into someone with resources, you have the ability to choose and actively participate in your life, and as soon as you begin to act you will realize it.

I am going to tell you about an experience that can help explain the importance of taking care of yourself, leaving aside worry. A great lesson that can be summarized as follows: *If you want to live an experience and feel that indecision or fear that brings you to insanity, do not even think about the steps you have to take, approach the cliff and ... jump!*

That past experience was about a jump, a paragliding jump in which I decided to confront one of my biggest phobias: vertigo.

During my last years in the Italian capital, I suffered from heartbreak, an experience I did not know much about. That grief left me quite moved. I felt completely stuck and I had lost great excitement in life.

Seeking to emerge from a great mental block in which I was in the midst of the inability to accept the loss of someone who had decided to follow a different path from mine, I felt the need to find drastic solutions that would help me change my perspective.

A few days earlier, my brother had made a paragliding jump with my brother-in-law. I had been invited, but due to the geographic distances that separated us, I wasn't able to join them. This fact encouraged me to try it, I needed to feel something different from that pain that ruled my days and the paragliding, could be a good choice.

I talked about it with my great friend Caruso, and fortunately, days later told me that he knew where we could do this activity near Rome.

I needed to do anything to help me get out of that state I was in, I knew from my own experience that the best therapy was a good attack. Facing with one of my fears could be my best medicine, so decided, together with Caruso and another great friend of ours called Roberto who would decide to join at the last minute, we organized everything necessary to face that great new and "therapeutic" leap.

I may seem like a strange person, but the worse I feel or have felt was when the need to live different or extraordinary experiences reappear in me, the cause may be in the intention of approaching life when you feel that you are moving away from it. At that time a good way to feel alive again could be, why not, achieve an impossible, and try to fly.

On the day of the jump, as we climbed the mountain in a van next to the monitors and the junk that would make up the wings, I realized what I was going to face. So far, I had never been able to lean quietly on the terrace of a third floor and, as we were told to climb that huge mountain, that flight, would start at a height of more than 1000 meters.

As we climbed the slopes of the mountain, I began to realize that in a few minutes I would live an experience that, had it not been for that depression that had me stunned, I would have never experience it.

The message I want to convey, the one I learned during that situation, I understood in the period that exists between the moment you know that you are going to face the jump and the moment you really start to run and you rush, the intervals that occur between the waiting and the action, the stunt that will bring you closer to what you realize you need to experience...

As we arrived to the top, the monitor who we would do the jump asked us the order of the jump. Since we were all scared and I knew myself too well, I chose to be the first to do it since I knew that if I did not, I probably would back down at the last moment. My friends accepted, so, scared and not fully understanding why I had entered this new madness, I prepared for this dreaded spin.

When we talked about the reptilian brain, we commented that the options before a possible attack to our survival were two: to fight or to flee. Faced with the challenge our body reacts automatically, I knew that before the possibility of escaping one of the reactions was to shit on yourself, something that I felt at that moment could possibly happen...

The purpose for which your body can give the command of shitting itself was to get us to smell so badly that the tiger or lion that our primitive brain considers to be attacking us supposes poisonous or even (depending on the odor) putrid and gives up in its action . In those minutes of waiting, my reaction was quite similar, my friends took a picture of me that really appreciates how, although not literally, my face made me realize that I was *scared shitless*.

With my face invaded by panic, I went to the hillside from which, in a few minutes, my flight would begin. Once there, it was time to wait since the jump was carried out by the monitor of a paragliding school and that day there were classes. In front of me and more than a thousand meters in height, different apprentices were ready to make the jump but, unlike me, they went alone.

While they were telling me how to run and move, and when I should start to do it, we expected these beginners (quite advanced when we consider the height they were in) to make their jumps; with the fortune in the form of misfortune that one of them made a bad flight and began to fear the worst.

After realizing what had happened my brain started to work only, I understood that I could die and in my head began to happen different possibilities in the form of images each more catastrophic. In my mind seemed to run a chapter of the series thousand ways of dying where I always appeared, my paraglider and the landscape in which I was.

Fortunately, a few minutes later, before he made the leap, they found that lad without any scratches and hanging between the trees; the news relieved me a lot, but the quiet was short-lived ... after a joke on the monitor, my concern continued to increase.

Joking (the expression on my face helped) along with my friends, the instructor explained how on one occasion, about fifty meters high before reaching the ground the moment you prepare for landing, a monitor released a kid-as I might be soon-directly into the void; his harnesses had not been tied tightly, and the innocent man was plunged. From that height it is not difficult to understand how it was all over, as you could imagine, did not survive.

After this anecdote that, after my feat, I would discover it was a joke, more images in my mind, so many and so apocalyptic, that my head was a complete chaos.

Accompanied by these thoughts, my monitor told me that the time had come, he was preparing to jump. I assured myself by asking as many times as I thought fit to tie my harnesses well, and, once we were sure, we prepared ourselves to do so...

Knowing that the time came and convinced of wanting to live 100% of what was about to happen, as if by magic I decided to eliminate the worries of my mind to focus on what occupied my present.

There was no turning back, some fifty meters separated life from possible death, the certainty of treading ground against the uncertainty of jumping into the void. The only thing I could and should do (hoping that what did not depend on me did not fail) was to run the best I knew as soon as my instructor, pilot, guardian angel and lifeguard told me.

I realized that there was no other option than that, I relaxed and prepared for action, soon I would enjoy my best career, I would do everything in my hands. And so it was, I ran and ran until there was no floor left, at which point I finally discovered the dreaded and amazing emptiness.

I survived and that stunt would become one of the most unique experiences of my life, a practice that I will do again as soon as I feel the need again.

With that jump I did not overcome vertigo, but I faced one of my fears whilst I realized that many times in life, worrying is nothing more than our imagination, fantasies that almost always serve as a pretext for not experiencing something that, like that jump, we want or feel necessary to live. It is necessary to overcome the fiction that raises our brain in the form of excuses to any challenge. Anxiety is a challenge for which there are no excuses, so, do not fool yourself, eliminate your "I can't".

When a challenge arises in your life, the brain usually tries to make you see the worst possibilities that can happen, excuses to stay in that safe and well-known area, our comfort space, a monotonous place where we can often feel dead in lifetime; it is in those moments when we must feel stronger, when we must fight to eliminate imaginary limits in our reality. Evolving is a change, because evolving as jumping, requires to put aside the excuses. We must get down to work to address what we really want or need to live, and even more strongly when we feel like the word illusion has become a distant memory.

Faced with anxiety we must do the same, it is time to eliminate any excuse. By now you know the path, you know the causes that your symptoms came to your life and you only need to make the leap. In the same way that it happened to me, you may have doubts and concern, but you need to do the opposite and convince yourself that you have everything you need. Once you feel and believe that your change is possible, happiness will accompany you in your days.

Feeling that you have taken the first step to embark your journey, will give you the necessary strength to enjoy the rest of the way. This is the reality of life; if you want it you can do it!

The best and the worst of anxiety is that, living with it, it leaves no room for half-measures. Its sometimes insufferable symptoms and the difficulty of leading a "normal life" make living with anxiety become unbearable; but it is in turn that struggle that helps us overcome it, since there are no other options to fight against what you feel to recover your long-awaited balance. Postponing, lamenting or avoiding is useless, that is why once we overcome it, we realize we have become stronger, someone with more resources for life, we have come to learn a great lesson

One of the greatest truths of this disorder that we are dealing with is that the sooner you take action, before your symptoms disappear, the simple fact of convincing yourself of it, of recognizing that you are adopting a fighting mentality, makes them diminish. If you still do not believe it, prove it yourself!

As I explained at the beginning of this writing, the important thing is that you take action. It is useless to accept the theory if you do not put it into practice. Your reptilian brain is smarter than you and, we have seen that sometimes, reason alone isn't worth anything.

To eliminate concern out of your life, you must relativize the symptoms, understanding that anxiety is not a terminal illness and that your ailments are as strong or weak as yourself. From your concern, you can make up your mind to feel them.

If you begin to see anxiety as a lesser evil that has come into your life to obtain a much more valuable asset, and accept that you can live with its symptoms without paying too much attention to them while you work on eliminating the reasons that originated them; if you relativize your anxiety and observe yourself better, you will be able to relax in situations in which you previously lost control and, like your anxiety, the symptoms will begin to diminish.

To be able to manage your mind and take action, you must prepare that great leap; by eliminating the concern from your present.

While you watch and prepare yourself, you will be attacked by your concerns, excuses and doubt. You will have to eliminate them because right now they are your worst enemy and, what is worse is that they are useless.

Think of your symptoms as an indicator that tells you what are the improvements that your life wants for you, and stop worrying. Keep your mind on that leap you are making, on your transformation; on how once you understand what anxiety is trying to tell you, your symptoms will disappear and you can enjoy the rest of the journey, *a better life than you had imagined.*

*Worry increases the intensity of your symptoms, your occupation is the best therapy, take care of yourself!*

## 3.6 Accept and discard, your life will begin to change

There is a before and after in the coexistence with this disorder, a moment that comes as soon as you accept that you do not suffer anything different from anxiety. At the same time that you discard other possibilities, your symptoms will begin to diminish. Your life will change and you will begin to feel a lot better.

Assuming anxiety does not mean giving up to it. Accepting it means understanding what your true problem is and understanding, consequently, what your true remedy is; in other words, be aware that you have the formula, *you are your own medicine*.

As I observed at that time and once back at ease, I could confirm that anxiety itself is not so bad. The problem of anxiety is in our excessive concern and fear of the unknown. If at the time, it came into your life you would have accepted the problem for what it was and you would not have given more value than necessary to each of its symptoms. I assure you that the intensity of these and their duration would have had nothing to do with what you felt or were suffering at that time.

Anxiety is the most common and universal of emotions. It is synonymous with anguish and worry about future events or situations of uncertainty. It is the fearful anticipation of imminent danger accompanied by an intense feeling of physical symptoms located in any region of the geography of our body. All of this gives us the feeling that something serious is going on to happen.

Believe it or not, life is inconceivable without it. A certain degree of anxiety is present in our lives on a daily basis. There is a normal desire, linked to the situations we live in, that fulfills an adaptive function and prepares the individual for the execution of tasks or alerts against possible threats and, there is another one that, far from helping us in life, makes it more difficult for us; the latter, also called pathological, leads to biochemical and functional changes in our body.

If when the pathological anxiety appears in our lives, and we accept it, we understand which steps to follow and start working to carry out this change, the symptoms will quickly disappear.

We can recognize this step as the first and necessary one to reduce the symptoms. Once you are really aware of it, you will realize that you feel better; from here, you will start the path that leads to recovery.

Imagine that you have a small boat and you have gone sailing, when a few meters from the port you bump into a great white shark that, out of curiosity, has approached a few meters away from you. Without a doubt you felt scared and tried to find a solution to your problem. You will realize that, not just *any* solution will work. There are millions of solutions but surely jumping out of your boat trying to scare the shark to punches is the worst of them. Treating anxiety without accepting it and believing from suffering other diseases would be doing the same. We would be entering the shark's land using tools that, far from hurting it, will make it stronger while you become weaker.

The time has come to accept it. To start walking along the right path. The only path that can help you recover the peace you need.

Starting from the basis of having accepted the anxiety, I will try to help you discover what our motives are, those for which that old-fashioned brain of singular name sounded the alarm, causing anxiety to appear in our lives.

*Accept it now*! You are only suffering from anxiety, you are not suffering from anything else. Smile, because you will soon discover that accepting the problem is a lot easier to overcome than you thought possible.

*Accept that you're not suffering anything different from anxiety, from that moment everything will start to change.*

# 4 Listen to what anxiety wants to tell you

*I freed myself of anything that is no good for my health- food, people, things, situations, and everything that drew me down and away from myself. They called it egoism, I called it "love of oneself."*
Charles Chaplin

*Know yourself!* Inscription found in the temple of Apollo in Delphi

Behind the different revelations that happened in my research, I began to recognize that the causes, the reasons why that disease came to my life and remained there, were inside me all along. An old brain had set off the alarm and, if I did not begin to recognize what my causes were and try to change the way I reacted to them, nothing would improve.

I knew I did not want to live controlled by anxiety, so I came to the conclusion that it was time to look within, it was time to get to know myself better.

Learning more in depth about our reptile brain, I discovered that, with the goal of survival, this organ was capable of generating not only diseases such as depression, stress or anxiety but also many others.

For this brain, the absence of illusion towards life, chronic boredom, or the feeling that the person in whom it resides in, follows a path contrary to his ideals or his possibilities. These are sufficient reasons to give us a feeling in the form of illness; to this brain, it is more difficult for it to maintain a continuous state of alertness, than to say enough and stop working.

Anxiety was just one of the ways in which this brain emits its orders by perceiving warning signals. Perhaps one of the mildest, a first warning that tries to help us to place ourselves in the right path.

During this time, I was very excited to be deciphering and understanding which were the reasons that had disappointed the intelligence with the name of a reptile, the same reasons that had made anxiety come in to my life.

I understood that my body was suffering and felt threatened by its own survival. This was enough to realize that the path I was taking at that time, was not the right one.

When you lose direction and you start going against life, life sends you signals to change. At this point you have two options, ignore them and change, or ignore them and continue living as if nothing happened. The problem with taking this second option is that you cannot go against life eternally; if you ignore the warnings for long, it will give you a wake-up call that you wo not have a choice but to stop to listen.

The time had come to change my perspective, to understand what was harming me and, from here, to begin to improve myself. Anxiety does not leave you with options, if you want to fight your symptoms, you have to do something about it, because if you do not, nothing will change.

When you realize it, and fight this disease with the true meaning and the true motivation that is to improve your quality of life, improving yourself as a person; you will begin (in the same way that it happened to me) to feel better, maybe better even than you felt before you had known about this disease.

Understanding anxiety, combating it, and slowly surpassing yourself, would not only make you stronger, but also a better person. You will become someone with more resources to life. The mission of your reptilian brain is to help you evolve, to help you understand that you are following a path that is taking you away from your happiness, from life that, if you really want it, you can choose to live.

After knowing the causes, effects and actors of this path that I was beginning to undertake, the time had come to carry out the most important, and perhaps most complicated exercise of all, to know myself better.

Observe your motives, eliminate what does not serve you, discard, test things out, change. Help yourself with the tricks that you consider necessary, run, breathe, and fight for moments of peace. Select your friends, your places, your situations better; define your interests, try and do different things, leaving aside the monotony. There are many actions you can take, you should look for those that make you feel better and bring you closer to life.

On that path that I had decided to undertake, it was time to take action, and the best way was to rediscover and bring to light that inner strength that we all carry within.

If you reread the quote that is at the beginning of this chapter, you will realize what I am talking about: *I freed myself of anything that is no good for my health- food, people, things, situations, and everything that drew me down and away from myself. They called it egoism, I called it "love of oneself."*

There is a medicine for anxiety, a cure that you will not find in any pharmacy, since it exists within yourself. I am sure you have heard about it, it is called *self-love*.

As we will soon discover in the next chapter, all the actions that we will undertake are based on reducing the sensations generated by anxiety. Those symptoms will be the compass that indicates the journey.

We must learn to be selective in our lives. Know what we want and who we want to surround ourselves with. Understand what makes us better and happier and let go of everything that does not; regain self-esteem so that, meanwhile we work on it, we realize that the world around us also changes.

If, for example, living with anxiety you spend your time with a cup of coffee or marijuana, it is easy for you to feel that your vertigos are growing the tachycardia increases and you feel worse every time; Anxiety is warning you that you are doing something that hurts you and, once you let go, you will begin to feel better, the same happens with our environment, people or lifestyle.

The symptoms of anxiety are the warning signs that indicate the path for change that help us recover our self-esteem. As soon as you act upon them, you will realize that you will begin to know yourself better. You will start to fight to improve the quality of your life.

Reducing and eliminating the symptoms of anxiety is a task as simple as doing what life wants for you and stop doing what you do not need and takes you away from your essence.

You can slowly face the problem or get straight to the point. Recognizing the reasons that affect you, the reason for your feelings, is to fight face to face, to listen to what the anxiety is telling you.

There will be external factors in your life (such as coffee, drugs, your environment, work, economy or condition) and other internal ones (thoughts, emotions or a sedentary lifestyle) that brought anxiety to your life, issues that if are not treated, they will keep coming back.

In my case, on that road that I was beginning to follow, I recognized that there were several battles I had to fight. Observing myself, and trying to perhaps for the first time (thanks to anxiety) know myself, it was time to recognize what my reasons were.

The moment I discovered that strange reptilian brain, I understood that drugs could have something to do with it, but once I accepted the message that anxiety brought to my life, I realized that there were many other reasons why my life was not quite right.

Aware of all this, I began to study myself, to study the effects of my thoughts and reactions to each of my symptoms. I paid more attention to the way I felt in the circumstances, not to the sensation itself but which was the cause that provoked a reaction in me.

Attempting to be objective with what caused my symptoms, this technique made me discover tools that would slowly bring me to that change that life wanted for me.

Above all, observing the highs and lows that my anxiety experienced before, the different external or internal circumstances in my life, I began to recognize realities like these:

- The concern, to associate my problem with other possibilities; that believing (sometimes) that my illness was different and closer to death or insanity, made me feel a lot worse. Focusing on my symptoms made them grow significantly.

- The vertigo made me feel insecure, I felt that I could fall at any moment, and thinking that it could happen in public places increased my anxiety. They rarely happened when I was at home, they were more due to a social factor, something external, and I observed that the problem was not in the situation itself but in my reaction to it.

- Playing doctor, and investigating my illness and associating it with different and worrying causes, increased my symptoms because focusing on them, made them bigger.

- Drugs, such as marijuana (the simple fact of smelling it even though I did not smoke it) caused my palpitations and my dizziness to increase, the effect was direct and imminent; with coffee it was more of the same, instant tachycardia's; alcohol could make me feel better at the time, but everything worsened the following day.

With drugs, not only did physical symptoms increase, but also psychological ones. Apart from these appearances, the lack of control generated by this unbalanced life, made me feel closer and closer to insanity.

- Public places, feeling with such little control over myself, made it difficult for me to go out to the street, to hang around the university or to perform tasks that I used to do with complete peace of mind.

- Socializing had become more complicated. I felt weird, I thought of myself as strange, and above all I thought that others could also see me that way. This feeling along with caring about the opinion of others, increased my anxiety.

- The negativity and the company of negative people generated more anxiety. Knowing and recognizing some of my difficulties, it wasn't time to bear more burdens. I must have begun to see colors in that world that lately looked so gray, I needed to see the light, and I needed to believe that it was possible.

- A sedentary life, not fighting against anxiety and having maintained a static lifestyle not only before but also during, did nothing to change my state. I couldn't sleep or think clearly, and standing still kept me that way, I needed to gain energy. Overcoming the anxiety required a lot of me, and turning into a lazy bear, would only get the opposite results.

- As for my friendships, I felt that part of those whom I had considered friends, were not at my side when I needed them the most. Some "friends" not only did not help me to try to even understand my situation but, worse, they made me feel more anxious and stranger than ever.

While I was working on getting to know myself, I began to recognize several of my causes until, taking small actions to change my reactions, I realized that I was beginning to regain control. The quality of my life began to improve, a better version of myself was born and, gradually reacting. I was realizing that I had the power to change everything.

Confident and determined, it was time to take action...

*The best medicine against anxiety is called "self-love", our symptoms will be our best compass to get it back.*

# 5 Smile, it is time to take action

*When you change the way you look at things, the things you look at change* Wayne Dyer

*The only cure for grief is action* George Henry Lewes

Past realities come to mind when I think about taking action. Experiences that, as the quote in which this chapter begins, happened thanks to changing the way I saw things. In this case, the way in which I understood my fear to change.

After living with anxiety, several incidents have showed me that if it is well treated, it neither conditions nor limits your life, but does the opposite. To explain how to understand and overcome this disorder, I'll tell you some of these facts.

A few months after overcoming anxiety, I did not think I would make a dream come true: *to live, discover and learn about Rome and its mysteries.*

After understanding the causes of my anxiety, I became a lot more motivated and encouraged to confront them, and to take action. Winning in self-love, the way of seeing and facing reality had changed. That new ¨me¨ would map out a plan to achieve a dream that I never considered possible to attain before.

After reading several books about this city, its mysteries and its empire, I informed myself about possibilities (they had always been there) that existed. The intention to understand its culture, learn its language, leave my city, live alone and discover the world, also helped.

I believed in myself, in life and in my good fortune; that was enough to generate and make a new reality possible.

I was so excited that, I found some scholarships called *Leonardo* to work abroad and managed to sign up for them. Fortunately, one of the possible options was Rome. As soon as I found out about it, I knew nothing could stop me.

Among the different requirements for the vacancies in Rome, the knowledge in certain subjects were requested, some of which I did not know, but I wasn't going to throw in the towel just yet. I believed in my possibilities, and so I decided to freshen up my resumé and make it as enticing as possible.

I understand and understood then, that life is about what you seek and how you intend to live it. The rules are sometimes meant to be broken, or simply be changed at your own risk (without the need to harm anyone).

After learning the requirements that were needed, I added other required education on my own and included a course (which I never completed) in my curriculum vitae in order to make it look more interesting. This was to present the best of the profiles to whomever had to choose the suitable candidate. I also falsified some other document that accredited the realization of a course of few hours (a small change that in case it was necessary, it would cost me very little to really learn).

I had accidentally become the perfect candidate and, a few days later, someone contacted me from Rome.

Once I was contacted, I knew that the opportunity couldn't get away so, using my best manners, education and intention, the possibility soon became a new reality.

In a few days a new chapter of my life would begin, an adventure that I lived and turned into a great experience that lasted or better said, I made it last, from the initial 4 months to more than 9 years.

To believe is to create and, believing in myself, I was able to make a dream come into reality. Working hard and encouraged by the stronger and wiser version of myself, after overcoming the anxiety that I once thought could end my life, I got to live unforgettable experiences. Among other things, I managed to learn a new language; get girlfriends and friends of different nationalities. I got to make a new culture my own, and got to discover an infinity of mysteries and live an endless number of new and extraordinary adventures.

The fact that I was able to put pessimism aside and take action, changing the way of thinking and doing something about it, I finally began to see results. Thanks to the anxiety, I learned about myself, and to change what was did not serve. From the moment I took action and took responsibility for my life and my circumstances, my reality, just like me, began to change.

Going back to my path, I remembered how my biggest fear those days was to think that anxiety could control the rest of my life. So, I am going to tell you something that I consider you should make yours for life; *knowing the importance of taking action and understanding what anxiety wants to tell you.*

I do not know if you know what agoraphobia is, but I knew her very well. So well, that I had her in bed for many days and nights.

My ex-girlfriend, the one who broke my heart, helped me among other things, like going paragliding. I knew I suffered from a problem, but I did not realize it until I began to live with her.

Agoraphobia can be roughly understood as fear of open spaces, going into more detail and having known it closely, is the fear of an environment in which the person who suffers does not feel safe.

I got a glimpse of my ex-girlfriend's problem when we did some daily tasks such as going to the supermarket or going out to dinner. Before any of these circumstances, she also suffered from nervous breakdowns that forced her (us) to return home.

Faced with that reality, I tried to help her by explaining that, from what I understood, the best way to attack the problem was when the symptoms presented themselves. Since it worked for me, I thought it could work for her too.

Soon I realized that my way of trying to help her, which was far from it, really got on her nerves. Faced with different and difficult circumstances such as leaving halfway through dinner to pay the bill and go home, the relationship was going downhill.

My help did not work and neither did the relationship, but I realized something important about the reality of that problem. Her agoraphobia, her panic attacks, were nothing more than an anxiety misunderstood and treated badly. The origins of her illness were very similar to mine, the difference was that she believed that the disease was stronger than she was and instead, realizing that it was the opposite and tackle the root of the problem.

In this way, anxiety had evaded her, she did not thing she was capable of overcoming it and felt like a victim of a problem with a difficult solution.

Without taking full responsibility for that first anxious outbreak, she took a lot of medication, which at the time did nothing but reduce the symptoms and never really eliminated them. Unfortunately, the anxiety controlled her life.

It is true that the state of imbalance in which we find ourselves leads us to afraid of life. Fearing for our harmony and sanity, but if we do not understand it or face it, we will feel incapable, weak, impotent, crazy or seriously ill, and there's where the problem lies. Feeling sick, considering ourselves different or unstable, we tend to get away from people to avoid feeling worse; to the point of, in very few cases, prefer to stay at home to avoid possible fainting and the subsequent will say, and thus avoid any kind of crisis. Believing to be impotent in the face of a problem that we understand as superior to ourselves, we leave our strength in the hands of anxiety and its symptoms.

The best advice I can give you is that understanding anxiety is necessary and that overcoming it is simple. You must not avoid it or fear it. If you avoid it, fear it or do not understand it, you will feel inferior, strange, sick and impotent and, surely choose medication and avoid therapy. This could be one of the worst decisions of your life.

From my experience, I can assure you that you can go back to living a great and even better and fuller life than you had before having known anxiety. To achieve it and be able to smile again, you simply must take action to overcome the problems that have led you to this condition.

Once you start working on changing, you will improve and eliminate things that do not serve you. Appreciating and realizing your change, you will stop fearing the possibility that anxiety may reappear in your life because you will have understood the message and why it has presented itself. Overcoming anxiety is as simple as this.

Understand the pain not as something mystical about what you have no capacity for reaction but as something that, now that you begin to understand, it can help you become someone better and stronger than you were or thought you were; someone with more resources for life.

Just as a caterpillar suffers in its period of metamorphosis to become a butterfly, anxiety has come to you to get closer to your true self, to your true path, so that you can stop feeling lost or helpless. You are responsible for what you feel and anxiety helps you take matters into your own hands.

The fear of the anxiety which controls you, comes only from the fact of not understanding it. At the beginning when we notice the symptoms, we believe that a deadly disease has come to us, we do not realize that it is only our body telling us that we need to wake up, we do not realize this need for change, but something that we have inside has decided to do it for us, and we must pay attention to it.

As you realize this truth, you will begin to take action on the matter accompanied by a new smile, a new and better version of yourself. The time has come to get down to work...

## 5.1 You are the butterfly, not the caterpillar

In my opinion, anxiety manifests itself more in people who over analyze things a lot. I am sure I think that way because I consider myself a good example of it; it also helps knowing that a lot of people whom I have known who have suffered or suffer from it, have a lot of me or I of them.

Something very common in people who suffer from anxiety is that, they usually look for a broader meaning in their lives; they are people who understand that life is something more than simply letting the days go by and letting go.

So if you want, and if you feel like it (I did it and it helped me a lot), feel different. Different but never inferior or even superior to those who do not value anxiety, or treat others who suffer it as if they were worthless. Think that in the animal kingdom there are certainly many who do not suffer from anxiety. It is very likely that it is because they have a smaller brain, so much that they do not perceive the change. They do not suffer from anxiety because they do not have the need to improve either.

If you feel that life is something different from what you have been told, if you feel that it is you who must discover the way to move forward, or simply feel there are things you would like to improve; feel special, feel different, feel better, because *You are the butterfly, not the caterpillar* .

Later on, (if you have not done so yet), you will notice that many of the people who suffered periods of change just like you, deserve more than many others who prefer to laugh at what they consider to be someone else's misfortune.

In this way the first form of action to fight anxiety will be to recognize it as a period of change, a metamorphosis that will make you a better person, and not see it as an illness or a weakness of which we are victims of.

Recognize in yourself someone special and even, if you want, someone better or more sensitive. Do not make the words such as: sick, crazy, weak or defective part of your vocabulary. In this period of change, we must maintain that smile that helps us improve ourselves. So, celebrate and feel it; feel these words I am telling you, and make them part of that new you. Continue smiling because the light is getting closer.

Once we understand the power we carry within ourselves, it will be time to attack this disease that tried to break us, by attacking our mistakes, *the reasons*, we will fight our symptoms back, and *the effects*.

As we already know, the symptoms detect the causes and at the same time, and no less important, they indicate the actions that we must perform.

We saw that in this disorder there are symptoms of different types: *physical, psychological, behavioral or social*. As with the symptoms, there is what we might call types of causes, *our own*. Causes that follow the same logic and that trigger these symptoms. To make it simpler I will include the most important ones in a short list:

- Responsibility towards life.

- Drugs or derivatives.

- Social phobia.

- People who are toxic.

- Negativity and worry.

- Sedentary lifestyle and dietary habits.

- Other factors...

These were some of the points that I was dealing with in which led my path towards anxiety. I remember that I did not create any list during that time, but I think that if I had made one, everything would have been a lot easier.

Guided by the compass of our feelings, we will begin to attack each one of our symptoms.

*Believe in yourself and begin to feel the change.*

## 5.2 The responsibility is yours

*There are two primary choices in life: to accept conditions as they exist, or accept the responsibility for changing them.* Denis Waitley

*Your life begins to change the day you take responsibility for.* Steve Maraboli

I am not a big fan of self-help books, since they tend to use complicated methods or they try to make the difficult things seem easy but, I must admit that between all of it, true and authentic works of art. If I had to choose one, I think I would choose *Your Erroneous Zone* by Wayne Dyer.

If one day you feel the need to make drastic changes in your life, you may like his book, but now is not the time. Right now you have to focus on your symptoms, improve and eliminate the pathological anxiety of your life and, as you probably know, doing several things at once does not usually bring good results.

Wayne Dyer's book is basically trying to make you understand, that a lot of things do not work in your life, simply because you are not really responsible.

 The erroneous areas of your life are due to the absurd amount of excuses that you put on yourself so as not to attack your problems. As the book explains, a lot of times we prefer to consider ourselves victims due to the tranquility and even benefits that makes us feel this way, rather than tackling the problem and recognizing that we are the only ones responsible.

This is the base of the chapter; you are responsible for your life, whatever you decide to feel depends only on you, recovering balance must now be your highest priority.

You might have thought that anxiety is stronger than you, but many other examples can certify that this is not true. I am sure that as you begin to make small changes in your life, your anxiety will begin to subside.

The first and most important of all change is that you are really aware that you are the only one responsible; only you can overcome anxiety, avoiding the issue will not help.

As you will see in the rest of the chapter, we will face different needs and, as indicated at the beginning of this book, this is a book about taking action, in which you are the main protagonist.

Anxiety is not something mystical or impossible, it comes to us with a specific purpose and its symptoms are related to our way of observing things. With all this, you can understand that the solution to the problem is not outside but within you. Feeling like a victim could have a single purpose, to live controlled by anxiety, which I imagine, you are not willing to accept.

Overcoming anxiety is as simple as you want to appreciate it and it doesn't depend on planetary alignment, some kind of witchcraft or universal justice. It is important to start seeing the world with different eyes and, within this new perspective, begin to appreciate that person in you with resources that you always had. Someone responsible for their reality, someone who is totally determined to improve their quality of life, someone with all the intention; otherwise, you would not be reading this book right now.

Being a responsible person, do not look for the solution to your problems in other people or acquaintances. A very common mistake

105

can create dependencies, relying on someone and believing that they feel more self-confident in their companionship.

Do not look for the answers outside; the responsibility is in you and the actions must be made solely on your own. Depending on someone exclusively will not reduce any of your symptoms. Although next to someone you can feel better, there is a life out there waiting for you, a world where sometimes, whether you want it or not, you will be completely alone.

If you only feel safe in the company of certain people, that can be a positive thing since, you are learning how to surround yourself with the right kind of people (as you will see later). However, avoiding other realities or using these people exclusively to face anxiety is not going to hide the problem.

Your life falters with anxiety, and this is why all of your actions must be directed towards one goal: recuperating balance.

If your stability depends exclusively on the support of other people and one day they go their own way, the punch can be a lot stronger, so learn how to fight alone; this is the best moment to do so.

Surrounding yourself with people who support you or encourage you to feel stronger is a wise choice, but overcoming your problems depends only on you. The causes of your anxiety are within you, the symptoms are your compass, the compass of a path that you must travel alone with. The responsibility of your anxiety is solely yours, therefore the changes must come from you.

*You are fully responsible for what you feel, the sooner you understand this, and the luckier will be.*

## 5.3 Say no to drugs

*Mens sana in corpore sano (A healthy mind in a healthy body).*
Sátiras de Juvenal

**Drugs are a waste of time. They destroy your memory and your self-respect and everything that goes along with your self-esteem.**
Kurt Cobain

Drugs and some of their derivatives, such as coffee or other stimulants, are substances with a direct and almost automatic effect on anxiety and its symptoms.

If you have trouble believing me and you live with anxiety, I encourage you to do a simple experiment, drink a cup of coffee and realize how in a few seconds, some of your symptoms increase without going any further, your tachycardia for example.

When drugs have such a direct effect, I think that it is one of the first things we must get treated. As soon as we do, we will notice a change, you will feel better since, part of the symptoms that bother you the most will have diminished or even disappeared.

I am not, nor have I ever been a saint. I am also not here to keep you away from experiencing or experimenting anything you want, far from it. I think that experimenting is the foundation of all learning because *you* must be the one who gives meaning to your actions and your world. You are the one who knows what you like and what you do not and, as I also try to be this way, one of the things I dislike the most is to judge or be judged. Therefore, whatever you do, I do not want you to feel doomed. I only want you to start taking action, and solve your problems.

In my case, experimenting and investigating directly within myself, I realized that most drugs did not suit me. I am still a weekend drinker but, apart from that, I do not use other drugs and I know I must thank the anxiety for that.

Whatever you may think about narcotics you should realize, and with this chapter I hope to help, that drugs (especially chemical drugs) affect your life and the way you feel. If you're not careful, certain drugs can make you feel that happiness be more and more complicated.

The brain is governed by chemistry, and happiness depends directly on it.

I am sure you know that if certain chemical components are mixed together they create reactions and, you have seen in movies or experienced in school laboratories how some of the reactions can cause real explosions.

With that in mind, we should easily understand that our body is not the best place to perform certain types of experiments with substances, often unknown.

Getting high is not very different from conducting a trial with one component, the drug, of which we probably have little or no knowledge of and even less of what the reaction will be in our body; for that reason, to play with some types of drugs can be similar to entertaining yourself with a time bomb, but the problem is that we live with this bomb, inside of us.

Chemistry plays a big role in the brain, happiness can be understood as a product of a thought that, when converted into a feelings, it becomes a sensation.

Overcoming a challenge, winning a prize, or seeing a loved one, no matter what it is, when you realize it, you feel (feeling associated with the thought of recognizing) something beautiful: happiness. Although chemistry is not tangible, you know it is always there.

When we feel happy, it is largely due to a series of hormones such as serotonin, dopamine or oxytocin that are secreted by our brain to transform thought into feeling. Serotonin and dopamine make us happier; not the fact that we are overcoming obstacles, winning a prize, or seeing a loved one; but the hormones that generate this sensation and, serotonin, like dopamine and many other hormones, are pure chemistry.

There are many hormones but, to summarize and help you understand the importance of brain chemistry, I will tell you about the ones that affect us most, for both good and bad.

There are three pleasure hormones:

- Serotonin affects serenity, optimism, concentration, self-esteem and stress.

 - Dopamine, the judge of the expectations that we have about things. A good outcome generates high levels of this substance increasing the sensation of pleasure. A bad outcome generates the opposite, and the sensation is not as pleasing.

- Oxytocin, is the hormone of love. It intervenes with falling in love, orgasms, maternal love and mating.

If our brain is able to secrete high amounts of these hormones, our happiness will increase, but if on the contrary by brain injury, disease, imbalance, genetics or other causes such as the use of drugs, the levels are not adequate. The predominant sensation will result in sadness.

Most drugs directly affect the segregation of these feelings that is why we feel happy after using drugs, we experience a sensation similar to an orgasm.

This demonstrates that drugs can affect our chemical imbalance, and just as with most things in life, going too far can make the opposite of what you want to happen. The reason is quite simple to understand:

Drugs can communicate to our brain the need to secrete hormones such as serotonin in an excessive amount. This association of narcotic-high, not only affects what we associate things with, but this sudden alteration with the drug, so we also become addicted to this substance to feel the same (psychological factor). It also affects the normal functioning of the brain, destabilizes it and, generally, the misuse of the drug causes the neurotransmitters responsible for secreting this or other hormones to stop working correctly, making the normal levels lower each time.

To be able to understand it better, think about the way you manage your savings, using drugs makes you squander like crazy, then you will be left with nothing and you will have to scrape your pocket, with the only difference is that, squandering with your happiness can bring many problems to your life.

You can understand that some drugs can daze you and others can make people who consume them very unhappy. The concern is that sometimes, they can transform for life.

In the case that you do consume drugs, you must understand that the use of many substances is directly associated with your physical and emotional state. The sooner you eliminate them either temporarily or permanently, the better you will feel and the more stable your body will be.

If coffee can affect your symptoms almost automatically, imagine the effect of stronger drugs such as marijuana, speed or cocaine.

This is your moment to take action, firmly convince yourself that, at least until you control anxiety and not vice versa, certain drugs have to disappear from your life. Your body is in imbalance and now is the worst time to perform certain types of chemical tests.

Before changing the subject and moving on to other topics, you will know or have been told that there are pills that are used to combat anxiety, they are called anxiolytics.

In my coexistence with this disorder, ignoring the process that I later learned (of which I speak in this book) I rarely used them, I soon discovered that I did not like its effects nor did they help at all.

After my first emergency visit, the doctor who treated me told me that these pills could help me fall asleep. I did not know, although I would soon discover, the new difficulty I would find in basic actions such as sleeping. That is why, that same night, I decided to use them.

I remember that in those days I read a lot to try to escape from that complicated reality. Among so many books I have read, there was a book that I loved, it was called One Flew over the Cuckoo's Nest, it told the story of a criminal who, preferred the psych ward than prison, and pretends to be crazy.

The story explained life inside the walls of a psychiatric hospital, it describes in a great way the different types of insanity. It helps you to understand that if you play with mental illness, you can crash and burn out. The protagonist of the story goes from being someone overly sane to a madly crazy person.

It was while I was reading that book that I began to feel the need to use those pills. Slowly, I realized that the effect of the painkillers was very similar to the description they made of the many mental patients when they were medicated.

I realized that anxiolytics can indeed calm you down but, the problem is that they do it so deeply that they literally leave you feeling groggy. If you have ever tried them, you will have noticed that the only thing left to do, was to drool.

I could be reading a book for hours without having understood or processed a single sentence until falling asleep and getting up the next day, with a sense of lethargy, which could have been caused by having slept five minutes as well as having done it for 15 days in a row. Due to these effects and other facts that caught my attention, I decided to stop using them. The other reason was that blur of a test to which I referred in previous chapters.

I did not need to wait for the drool to fall to realize (although I had trouble sleeping and it was difficult to cope with the symptoms) that it was better to leave the pills aside.

Convinced, I decided to eliminate the anxiolytics from my life. I would only use them on occasion- I will talk about it in the *tricks of during* chapter-, to feel more self-confident.

If you can accept a piece of advice, I would suggest you stop using any type of drug that affects your present state nor abuse the medications and take them only in case of maximum need. Understand that you are stronger and that, if you need it, nature has much healthier medications such as running, sex, chocolate or having a chamomile tea, which will not make you fail any exam, or drool while you read without even reading.

Going for a run, surrounding yourself with positive people, watching a good movie, or having good sex, are much better and lasting medicines and, above all, will make you overcome anxiety without conditions or dependencies. Believing that the solution is exclusively in those substances such as anxiolytics is not an intelligent thought.

In this chapter we will eliminate everything that directly affects your symptoms, you will easily discover (you should start now) that drugs are the most direct factor of all in that imbalance you are feeling.

*Say no to drugs and you will quickly feel better.*

## 5.4 There is a plant that can help you

I am sure you have understood that drugs, especially in these moments, are best to be left far away. If you are (rather, you were) a fan of some kind of plant, there is no doubt that was the reason this chapter caught your attention.

It may sound strange to you that after I was being very blunt, and told you to *Say No To Drugs*!, I talk to you about a plant that can help you, but that is right, this plant with miraculous properties is called *Hypercom* and in countries like Germany, it is considered a medicine sold in pharmacies to treat different types of disorders, among them, anxiety.

Hypercom, also known as St. John's wort, can be purchased normally in herbalist stores. They come in different formats or solutions such as pills, drops or infusions; if you thought about smoking it, I am sorry to tell you that this plant cannot be smoked.

I encourage you to challenge yourself today, and look for an herbalist store nearby and get it.

I hope I have helped you to understand that drugs or medicines like anxiolytics, far from helping you to fight anxiety, usually have the opposite effect. We could understand these tranquilizers as a medicine with short-term effect, and that is why in some cases they are prescribed. They have an effect similar to an anesthetic dart; a pill of this "drug" manages to eliminate anxiety for a while but, *Caution!* It also takes away your energy, your vitality and spirit, making you feel dead in life. The goal of anxiolytics is to eliminate anxiety by making you sleepy, so if you want to lead a normal life, both any medical professional and I, and even you - if you have ever used them - will tell you that it is not the best solution, in fact, it is not even a solution.

To make the anxiety disappear, it must be treated and there is no medicine that makes those changes for you. You must take action and to help you with it, the *Hypercom perforatum* can be a good ally.

This plant is also known as the plant of joy or the grass of light and the nickname of Saint John's Wort is that its flowering period began on June twenty-fourth, the day of the Saint, the date on which the summer and light and joy come outs. With these nicknames, it is easy to get some affection.

Its use comes from ancient times, and in Ancient Greece it was believed that it had magical properties and was used to expel demons, it was also believed that it could attract love and guarantee happiness and health. There are many properties from this plant that have to do with health, more specifically it has a direct effect on mild depression and anxiety, the main objective of this book.

Since it is an all-natural medicine it has no harmful effects, so it is usually prescribed for cases of discouragement, sadness and anxiety and it is said to overcome shyness.

Regarding anxiety and depression, it has been discovered that *Hypercom* (from studies carried out by international health agencies) exerts a tranquilizing effect and helps to balance the nervous system of the person consuming it, helping them to sleep better by increasing the levels of melatonin and calming anxiety, without altering or inhibiting sexual desire or cognitive ability (unlike anxiolytic tablets).

I got to know this plant in some of my anxiety stages and, without understanding why (it was probably due to its healing properties) I felt like using it gave me the boost to help me know what my life commitment and my needs are. Making these actions bring me closer to change, and to balance.

As I mentioned before at the beginning of this chapter, challenge yourself. Do not hesitate. Introduce the Hypercom in your life and feel its effects while you continue helping yourself while reading this book to achieve your goal, this herb can give you the impulse you need to carry out the actions that will bring you closer to what life wants for you.

You will understand that overcoming anxiety or any challenge that life poses to you depends solely and exclusively on you, so if you use Hypercom or any external "help", always remember that it is and will be a support, never the solution. Nothing and nobody (not even this plant) should control your reality, so if you introduce the *Hypercom* in your life do it as a boost, once in motion, you can leave it whenever you want, and you will not need it.

In any case, this herb can be a valid medicine to treat some of the discomforts produced by anxiety but it is not essential. Overcoming anxiety depends solely and exclusively on your actions and you can achieve it without having to resort to any kind of external aid. Think of the Hypercom as a vitamin restorative that can provide strength in case you feel your need, the rest always depends on you.

*The Hypercom can give you strength to make you seem livelier in each of anxiety's symptoms.*

## 5.5 Learn to relativize, and reduce your social phobia

*The moment I started treating my social anxiety disorder, I started to feel better.* Ricky Williams

*The eyes of others are our prisons, their thoughts our cages...* Virginia Woolf

Among the many symptoms of anxiety, the lack of balance is perhaps one of the most common, the most controlling and bothersome of them all. Maybe you have not noticed yet but this feeling is almost exclusively when we are in public, think about it and try to remember, I am sure this has happened to you.

One of the ways to easily understand that anxiety has a physical and a mental part, is to think about how and when some of its symptoms are presented; for example, dizziness and vertigo.

In my case, this and other sensations worsened as soon as I left the house, walking down the street, in the university, the bus. I began to feel an imbalance that made me constantly feel dependent to everything.

Accepting the vertigo I realized that the mental part, the worry, that fear of feeling anxious recognizing our imbalance, did nothing but increase the power of the symptoms, why it is very easy, suffering anxiety we do not feel safe and being alive we have to live inside, but also outside the home, where we are not always so comfortable.

The trick to controlling many of the protests of the disorder, is to eliminate unnecessary burdens or anxieties. As we saw in previous chapters, the belief that you can suffer a more dangerous condition makes us feel even worse, all this is generated by the mind, and it is easy to understand that in the case of suffering a really serious illness the mental factor would have nothing to do with the physical symptoms.

We live in an internal imbalance generated by one of our brains and if we feed him more fears we will feel worse, moreover, if we believe that these fears are real, we can end up conditioning the rest of our lives.

Vertigo is not due to anything different than our lack of self-confidence that we feel when living with this imbalance. Being with other people that we consider "normal" and recognizing ourselves "unstable, weak or defective", we breathe more quickly, our pulsations are accelerated and every time less blood and oxygen comes to the brain, all this causes us the feeling of vertigo and makes us think that we can faint. This last sensation increases social phobia, we may think; What if I faint, what will they think of me? Or, worse, we may not even think about anything and only realize that staying at home with our partner or family these things do not happen, and we prefer to avoid going out.

There is only one question, do you want to live isolated from the rest of the world?

You know that if you want to live a full life, the answer is *no*.

I know you want a happy life, and you deserve it, so try to identify that the cause of your social phobia is due to the increase of your symptoms and learn to manage them. Give less importance to situations, people and circumstances, understand that what you suffer has a name and recognize that the best solution is the direct relationship between the burden and its symptoms.

Sweating, tachycardia and hyperventilation, generate your vertigo and everything is in your head, due to your feeling overwhelmed because you feel different, or you do not feel safe. It is very important that you understand and begin to change your approach to certain circumstances that you recognize that upset you. You are not sick nor are you different, and above all you are no less than anyone. Everything is in your thoughts and you can control these thoughts, improve, and even change them.

If you have not understood the last paragraph, it is important to reread it. *If we do not understand that many of the symptoms of anxiety are generated by ourselves due to the way we feel in different situations, we can become slaves of the problem believing that what we feel does not depend on ourselves and we do not have the power to face it or change it. There is nothing mystical about your symptoms or reactions because everything started ... inside of you.*

You choose which path to take in the face of anxiety, the healthiest and simplest is to realize that you are in control, not anxiety.

We must learn and introduce a new and important mental skill in our lives. We need to learn how to relativize.

*"Relativize: Giving something less value or importance than what we give it."*

Begin to use this word as far as anxiety is concerned. Anxiety does not kill you, it is temporary and its symptoms grow when we focus on them. The less importance we give them, the smaller they will be. So, acknowledge it and begin to take action on the matter.

The secret to fight against this craving now and in any occasion that may arise, is to give less value than we give. Understand that anxiety is only asking for a necessary change, which is nothing definitive or deadly, and we should only take action (it is no use worrying) to see the change we are looking for.

I do not know if you have ever suffered from a broken heart, if so, you may have realized that what hurts is not moving from love to hatred, the real pain brings indifference.

Indifference kills any feeling and what you suffer for now is due to what you feel. If, in a social situation, your fear lies in what people say or think about you, the time has come to change your way of thinking.

Start by being indifferent to some symptoms and what certain people may think of you. Relativize your temporary problem by being happy and observing that you are changing.

For example, when you get on a bus full of people and begin to feel sweaty, your heart is pounding or any other symptom, observe yourself and recognize what you are feeling. Observe the way your mind creates your symptoms and, when you realize it, perform some activity that brings you back to being calm. In chapter six, you have some exercises that can help you achieve this. You can find one that can help you and start working for you.

If you apply indifference and the art of relativizing to those social situations that generate anxiety, you will see that the effects diminish, your self-confidence grows and you begin to observe the direct influence that you have on your symptoms.

A period in your life has come, in which you will learn to give the right value to things, people and situations. Your symptoms are telling you all of this and you should listen to them.

Relativize and observe how in a few days you can coexist with anxiety, learn from it and overcome it to the point of not fearing it, of living with or without it so that you do not worry that it can continue or return to your life again.

When I was faced with anxiety, I learned to observe myself, I recognized the way in which these changes occurred in me; when the symptoms came up, something warned me and in this way I learned to treat them. I had the key to put my mind at peace, and with it I also realized the causes of my imbalance. Acting on my symptoms I began to feel better and better learning to react in a way that would make my life a lot better.

In the period of your metamorphosis, in your process of personal growth, you will realize that you must deal with many difficulties; working on overcoming them, you will be feeling better and stronger and this feeling will become your best ally while you still live with anxiety.

Do not avoid social situations, only learn to control yourself and control them, you are not crazy, or terminally ill and you are not a weak person, you are only changing.

*Start by caring less about what you are feeling, and soon you will feel better. The symptoms get worse when we focus on them.*

## 5.6 Avoid toxic people

*A real friend is one who walks in when the rest of the world walks out.* Walter Winchell

*A man is a Wolf rather than a man to another man.* Pluto

They say that true friends recognize themselves in bad times, and you will soon realize the great truth that life will later show you.

In the face of adversity or problems, many people prefer to run away than to invest time or energy in helping you. Those who stay by your side in the most difficult times are the people you should not let go of; personally this is one of the secrets to enjoy a better life, learn to be selective with the people who enter it, it is not enough to just accept, we must choose.

With anxiety you will learn to support, conserve and value who really deserves it; you will become more selective and believe me, few things are as important as knowing how to choose the people who accompany you along the way.

Being social animals we can find a good simile in nature. To give you an example, I will talk about the gazelles.

Imagine that you are one of these animals and that, running to escape a hare that you confused with a lion, you stumbled and broke a leg. Before your incident many gazelles were having fun by your side. You had many friends and a great family, we could say that these were "your pack of gazelles".

After the incident, both you and your environment have recognized that you have a problem. Maybe you do not have time to regret your luck or your mistakes, or maybe you do, but what is certain is that you recognize that your life is in danger (with anxiety your life is not in danger but your present has become much more complicated), you know that you need to get back in to the best conditions to get back to running as soon as possible since, there are lions out there and if you do not run, it is easy to soon become part of their daily menu.

Faced with the difficulty and change, negativity will flood your life, you will feel dejected and, you will begin to realize that who you thought were a part of "your pack of gazelles", move away from you.

Similarly, you have brought this upon yourself. A good part of them will continue to be on your side waiting and encouraging you to recover and enjoy the mentality and vitality that you had before suffering this altercation. It is also possible that new comrades may approach you, with the sole intention of helping you out.

Some of those that used to support you will follow the herd without waiting for you to recover. They will leave you because they feel more secure along with the rest of the "gazelles without problems", even if there is one that you consider a lost cause or laugh at your problems.

Those who leave will find different excuses, who will simply want to continue enjoying the benefits of following the herd and their safety. Others will feel bored of listening to your problems and there will be those who simply prefer to enjoy their luck and leave that poor gazelle aside that you have become.

You will discover others that will not only leave you behind, but will try to put more salt in the wound, making you feel weaker and misunderstood, a race of the worst kind. It will be difficult for you to understand the reason for so much evil, but they do exist, they are subjects who, faced with their feelings of inferiority, only feel important attacking their peers; in this way they believe to instill fear or respect and this is the sad way they have to defend themselves against possible attacks. These gazelles feel lame without being and although attacking, are always on the defensive, you should not fear them or ignore them as this would make them stronger, this type of subjects should only be ignored when understanding the smallness of their reality since, think about it, *who may need to attack or despise a fellow person to feel big or important?*

For this, if someone attacks you, hit them with indifference; it will be the karma that one day will make them realize that mental lameness by putting them in their place.

People are animals and as happened to the crippled gazelle, we need to choose the people who support us, who listen and stay at our side, whatever the circumstances. Beings that will help this path called life to be the most beautiful and peaceful possible.

Anxiety, is that temporary limp that you are suffering. It is the perfect moment to help you recognize which people are worthwhile and which are better to leave aside. The sooner you put distance between the people who complicate the present and complicate the future, you will be able to run again and above all, the period of rehabilitation will be less hard.

Those people who encourage and defend you, those who understand you and listen (although sometimes it can be difficult), those who suffer or cry by your side, those who wait for your leg to improve to run again together and even help you fight a lion if necessary, those are the people you need by your side now and always; and now is the best time to realize it.

Before my being crippled (my anxiety), I learned to recognize who were the important people in my life and who were not. My symptoms helped me to understand it and recognizing these indicators I began to be more selective choosing the type of friendships I wanted by my side.

With that first anxiety experience, I was able to get closer with my real friends, and get rid of the fake ones. It freed me from people who affected my physical and mental state. Beings that poisoned the present, people we might consider toxic.

In the face of anxiety you will see how some of those you considered friends, do not want to listen to you, embarrass you in public, laugh, making you feel weak or simply ignore you and your problem; you will realize that with these people your vertigo and your social phobia increase and other symptoms get worse.

Faced with the need to have peace, anxiety leads us to the way and, in this path, it teaches us that cutting your losses will make for a better life.

As with drugs, toxic people affect your life. If, along with certain people, your symptoms become more acute, recognize this warning, be aware of the people you have in front of you; if it is their way of behaving with you that increases your anxiety, and realize that it is time to avoid them.

If one of those people are a very close relative or someone whose commitment you cannot get away from, try to see them as little as possible and protect your mind from your thoughts. Do not let it affect your reality or your way of appreciating the world.

If you continue down this road, you will begin to be more selective with the people that are part of your life, during the time you are experiencing anxiety, you will realize it and, you will slowly have this capacity of selection into a new and important virtue that will be with you for the rest of your days.

Keep on contemplating this sign and see how you continue to improve while you get stronger and stronger, you are beginning to relativize your symptoms, to be indifferent to what they will say and more selective with everything that has a direct effect on your mood. With or without pain you still feel that anxiety has an objective and, realizing this reality, you feel how your symptoms are disappearing while your self-love continues to grow.

Along the way, this message of improvement that anxiety brings to your, life should be burned in your mind to never disappear. It is not enough to understand the theory if you do not put it into practice. So, if you can start today, and be more selective with the people that are a part of your life.

*You should be the one who chooses which people are a part of your life along the way. Learn how to recognize "your people".*

## 5.7 Think positive

*Whether you think you can or think you can't, you're right.* Henry Ford

*It is not what happens to you, but how you react to it that matters.* Epictetus

A great value that brought anxiety to my life was discovering the importance that thoughts have in our lives.

Today I am increasingly aware of this truth: we design our life and what we create depends on our ability to believe in ourselves, actively shape our reality. The probability of making any dream come true, depends directly on the intensity with which you believe you can make it real.

For our reality to be as fascinating as possible, there may be nothing more important than this: *to improve and control what we think about.*

The way in which we approach our judgments and the way in which we manage our experiences have a direct effect on our reality. Henry Ford's quote in which this chapter begins with, illustrates this idea perfectly: if you do not believe in something, even though your surroundings are indicating otherwise, you will wait for any sign to confirm your belief. Whatever it may be, make sure you are right.

*Now* is the best time to imagine a better life, the time has come to try to improve our thoughts.

In the past, when I lived with anxiety, everything seemed dark and gray. I feared for my mental health without finding an outlet and worse, I thought that maybe there was not an exit. In those days, I felt that my life had changed forever.

Like in a vicious cycle; negativity, mistrusting and blaming the world, made me isolating myself from others. It is easier to blame your bad luck or the time you have lived, "dodge the issues" believing that nothing depends on you, to take responsibility for the reality in which you find yourself and fight to change it.

You have two options: to continue feeling like a victim and nothing changes or change your life modifying your way of thinking and taking responsibility for it. The choice is yours, but the anxiety and your symptoms will not improve while you decide to play the victim. On the contrary, the sooner you decide to commit to your life, the sooner your reality will change.

If you still think that the problem is not your own, understand that the difficulty will not disappear by itself; if on the contrary you understand that only you can change things and you get to put in the work, before you know it, things will change too.

All in all, anxiety is about making us learn to accept that we are directly responsible for our lives. The anxious goblin asks us for a change of path, habits, friendships, and thoughts. Since that old you receded from what your life really wanted for you.

We must help ourselves from Epictetus' well-known phrase to understand it, *it is not what happens to us that causes sadness, but what we say to ourselves about what has happened.*

If we decide to think that anxiety is an unresolved evil that has come to our lives to torment us, that bad luck and this cruel world has been primed with us, or to use like thoughts, we will be sending a message to ourselves that there is no way out and that there is no solution. We will feel sad and dejected, defeated and without possibilities and, in this state, we will not try to open our eyes to find

If you complain about the world, about life or about bad weather, now that you suffer anxiety or before it reaches your life, it is time to change that way of thinking; whether you want to understand it or not, you will not go anywhere like that.

The correct option is to choose to identify ourselves as fighters and to fight, it is not important how many times we fall but how many times we get up.

If you start by seeing that there is a fighter inside you, whatever your cause may be, this force will not only make you overcome the problem but even further, it will help you use, know and recognize capabilities in you so that any problem that comes to your life, instead of throwing in the towel, fight and work until you solve it.

You can decide right now to send yourself this message: Anxiety has come to me because I needed to change certain aspects of my reality and fighting and being responsible for what happens to me, I am leading to a better and fuller life. In short, *there is a bright side to everything*

If you start to take responsibility for your life and decide to adopt this new way of thinking, each day that passes by, you will be getting stronger; acknowledging it will not only make you better at combatting the difficulties of life but also make you feel and discover within you that you are a better person.

There is no better ally in your struggle than to help you with good thoughts, so find a way to eliminate negative thoughts from your mind, fight them. A good trick is to recognize them when they arrive, tell yourself that you have had enough of thinking like that, and attack them instantly.

Changing your thoughts is not an easy task, but if you identify them and begin to work with them, you will begin to accept that your happiness depends almost exclusively on the way you manage your mind. You will begin to observe that you feel bad most of the time because without even noticing, that is what you have decided in your head.

We feel what we think and happiness is a feeling. Believe it or not, thoughts have much more power than we can imagine and the following experiment will definitely help you understand it better.

## An experiment: the effect of thoughts

To help you understand the importance of thoughts in your life I will tell you about a surprising investigation that you may not know.

A few years ago a Japanese scientist named *Masaru Emoto* conducted an experiment whose amazing results brought very important message for humanity.

To carry out the study, the doctor used two ingredients: one was water the other, although it may sound weird, the thoughts.

It seems strange that thoughts can be used in an investigation since they are not something tangible but *Mr. Emoto* would show that, although the thoughts are not material, if they have the capacity to transform the physical elements, his experiment would prove it.

To perform the test the doctor labeled bottles of distilled water using and sticking labels with different expressions, some recipients associated them with positive phrases such as Love, Gratitude, or Wisdom and in others, used negative terms such as Hate, Fear or Insanity.

During the time the investigation, a number of people interacted with the exposed bottles by sending them thoughts related to the expression they observed on the label.

After the process, *Dr. Emoto* evaluated the results obtaining water samples from each container identifying, separating and cataloging their molecules, the results would be surprising...

When photographing these molecules with an ultra-microscope, he discovered how water, its shape (at the molecular level) reacted to the thoughts that had been applied to it. The untreated distilled water had no form, while the water to which the thoughts were applied reacted by adopting extraordinary forms.

If you search the internet, you will see the images and the different experiments made by this Japanese scientist. You will definitely be surprised.

The message of this research is clear: *if thoughts can do this to water, imagine what they can do to us.*

We know that our brain is chemical and that 90% of our body is made up of water. This experiment has shown that water reacts to thoughts, so understand that thinking in a positive way is much more important than you could believe because, whether you want it or not, the way you think also affects your health physical.

Whether it is difficult for us to accept it or not, if we react physically to thoughts, we can understand that many diseases and problems could be avoided if we learned to treat ourselves better.

Accepting this truth is even more important if you live with anxiety, since the effect of your thoughts directly influences the symptoms of your imbalance.

Once again, you know that you must keep fighting to recover your best circumstances and one of the most important actions is to improve your way of thinking, on our way to overcome anxiety is almost an obligation to be more positive and, the sooner we start doing it, we will feel better

Both in these cases, and in the rest of difficult moments that you will have to suffer, negativity can become a habit that takes you away from your goal. Overcome your problem and understand the change you must experience.

You can see negativity in many places, people or situations but, if you improve your thoughts you can avoid associating darkness with those circumstances. As far as people, they can be a little more complicated...

If among your group of friends, you find other people surrounded by negativity, it is time to get away from them or avoid them. Consider this stage as a stage of inner cleanse in which it is mandatory to improve your way of thinking.

The more you smile and appreciate your inner strength, the greater your joy will be. The more joy you feel, the less energy they will adopt to your symptoms. Therefore, although anxiety makes it difficult, now is the moment to feel more alive than ever.

Whatever your motives are, do not accept that the problem is in the world or in life. Life is never entirely fair, but think of justice for the poor gazelles constantly attacked by lions.

The Latin proverb "Post nubila Phoebus" indicates that after the storm the sun rises. Use this proverb in your life at any time of difficulty, and in this case, this is one of them. Recognize that everything will improve, you may need an umbrella to repel the rain (negative thoughts or relationships) and to see the sun again; one of the best solutions is to go to that sun and, as you will discover in the next chapter, if you run after it, you will get there faster.

*Your thoughts create your reality, start to control your way of thinking and soon you will see how the world around you also changes.*

## 5.8 Mens sana in corpore sano

*Insanity is doing the same thing over and over again, and expecting different results.* Albert Einstein

*Running is one of the best solutions to cleanse the mind.* Sasha Azevedo

As Einstein's approach well explains, for our lives to change we need to change our habits because if we always do the same thing, we will obtain similar results.

Maybe the good or bad luck that many people associate with destiny, zodiac signs or planetary alignment, depends only on what we do with our life and, I am sure that taking responsibility for your own destiny will bring you much better luck than being a Virgo, Christian, Muslim, or a magician's apprentice.

One of the most important things you can do to enjoy a healthy life is to practice sports. Any activity that we should make a frequent habit in our lives. To understand the importance of practicing sports, we can find a great example in a one of the best movies in time: *Forrest Gump*.

I imagine you already know the story of this movie, otherwise I encourage you to see it as soon as you can, you will feel better, you will win in positivity and maybe you will also be encouraged to run aimlessly and without destiny. Personally, it is one of the best movies I have ever seen and definitely one of the best ones which mix drama, comedy and motivation in a surprising way.

In the film, actor Tom Hanks gives life to the character *Forrest Gump*, an extraordinary human being that in spite of the difficulties that life put before him in the same moment in which he was put in this world, was able to live a full and extraordinary life. Although it is a fiction movie, its messages are totally real, messages that adapt to our own lives would certainly make it much more extraordinary.

The message of the film could possibly be this: *It only depends on you to obtain everything you want from life, you create your own reality with your actions no matter what bumps you find along the way.*

*Forrest*, literally fighting against all odds, managed to live and experience all that he wanted; He found his own methods and one of the methods that helped him the most was simply *running*.

After one of the most difficult moments of his life, the death of his mother and the abandonment of his beloved, *Forrest* realizes that he has no goals or illusions to help him overcome the problem; before such a dilemma and without thinking twice, he begins to run aimlessly, without direction or goal. *Forrest* quickly understood that there was no better remedy to eliminate worry than to take care of himself.

Instead of turning things around and spiraling, he began to run until some time, and a few thousand miles later, he had an idea that made him stop. He had just found a new goal, a new dream that could return his smile.

When we live anxiety we have a clear objective, stop feeling their insufferable symptoms to enjoy a healthy life.

In our struggle, running, walking, or doing any type of physical activity, is definitely one of the best means and remedies to return to enjoy a full life. We already know that turning the symptoms around does not solve anything but quite the opposite so, instead of investing time in vain investigating possibilities that do not exist, take advantage and just *go for a run*.

Exercise optimizes our energy, it regulates our body, cleanses our mind and perhaps the most important thing: it is the best antidepressant that nature has devised for human beings.

It is proven that running is one of the best natural antidepressants and that drugs or anxiolytics at this time do not help us at all, rather resort to nature than to new and unknown drugs that can do you good today but very bad tomorrow.

Once again, anxiety leaves us with no other solution than to take action. The sooner you start, the sooner you will know its meaning and the sooner it will disappear from your life.

As with *Forrest Gump*, worrying set me in motion and since then, running several times a week has become one of my favorite habits.

To encourage you not to wait until tomorrow I will tell you some of the benefits it can bring to your life by telling you some of the ones it brought to mine:

- An imminent effect on your mood, you will immediately feel better when you notice that the symptoms of your anxiety are reduced.

- Exercise helps to control your mind and to organize your thoughts, if you have a problem, run or perform another type of physical activity will help you find the best solution; *sports and exercise clarify ideas.*

- You will like yourself more and immediately will be liked by others and will be able to flirt more.

- You will have more energy and whatever your age, or what condition you are in, you will be in a position to perform many tasks that you previously considered impossible.

- You will sleep better and you will cleanse inside and out. Your body circulation will improve, so will your skin and even your dreams (in the case that you may have some difficulty to sleep) will be pleasant as when you were a child.

- You will lose weight, approaching your ideal weight.

- You will learn to be more tenacious in life, gaining will power.

- You will have better sex.

- You will realize that you are responsible for your life.

These are just some of the benefits that exercise will give you, so do not think about it anymore, if you need to buy shoes, make this your highest priority, you know that anxiety does not wait and needs results. The sooner you recognize them, the sooner you will stop being upset.

Maybe you have always led a sedentary lifestyle or maybe the difficulties and incomprehension that you have felt have let you down. In this book I try to help you realize that you are the only one responsible for what you feel right now. The only person responsible for what you will feel tomorrow as well.

Life is not going to change if you do not change. You will not feel better while you spend hours on the couch lamenting and food (sometimes junk food) fills your little moments of happiness. With anxiety, you have two options: do nothing, continue with it and feeling controlled by it; Or, look for good running shoes and go out for a run to make the storm pass and you can enjoy the sun as soon as possible. You decide, the responsibility is only yours.

The biggest difficulty of tying up the shoes and going for a run has a name: reluctance, but to fight it there is a very simple trick, be faster than it. As soon as something inside you tells you to leave it for tomorrow, recognize it, put on your shoes and go out the door without thinking twice (do not forget the keys). A few steps later you will feel better and the apathy will have disappeared completely. If your schedule allows it, I encourage you to do it right now and observe the results.

I talk about running because personally it is the exercise that makes me feel better once it is done. However, any type of sport will help you fight and reduce the symptoms of anxiety, improving your quality of life.

You can run or walk, play football, paddle, surf, bike, squash or any sport that exists. You can even invent one if you want; there are no excuses of age or what kind of shape you are in, if you want to use this excuse, I encourage you to look for a sport that suits you. If you believe that it does not exist, you are deceiving yourself; walking, swimming, cycling, doing push-ups or aerobics can be your solution because, just as with movies in the cinema, there are sports for all ages.

If the reluctance still exists in you, there is no problem, you can run with it, set an initial goal of 30 minutes 3 days per week, whatever the activity is and, whether at a mile per hour or a hundred. Overcome your challenge and watch how you feel; once you have exceeded your goal, your reluctance will have diminished, you will feel happier and more eager, your symptoms will lose their bellows and your head will begin to believe more and more in your possibilities.

Stick to exercise, understand its strength, understand yours, and make sports your faithful companion. I assure you that if you practice it regularly for at least a month, many of your problems will have diminished and your anxiety will have been reduced considerably.

If drugs increase the symptoms with a direct and imminent effect, practicing sports does the opposite. It decreases them directly and automatically.

Before the exercising, before that new you that is born within you, your brain is realizing that you have understood the message and you work on it, your metamorphosis has begun, and believe it or not, you will soon reap the fruits; you will soon feel the great outcome.

Physical activity will improve your life, but perhaps your health should also be accompanied by another important ingredient: *healthy eating habits.*

Foods such as fried or carbonated drinks can have an effect similar to that of drugs in your body, while limiting the energy needed to carry out beneficial actions such as exercise, reluctance can be caused by embarrassment or bad food among others.

If you see that your eating habits have gotten worse, after dealing with anxiety, recognize these bad habits and change them. You may not have noticed but, eating impulsively can be one of your unconscious reactions to anxiety and if you want to understand it or no, this affects your balance.

If your intestine is more closed than usual, pay attention to foods that can cause constipation such as excessive rice, fried food, saturated fat or industrial pastries; do yourself a favor, reduce them or eliminate them from your life.

Understand that what you eat not only affects your physical state, it has been shown that foods such as fruits or vegetables and fish produce mental well-being that cause anxiety and symptoms to be reduced.

If the new or recovered you can control what enters your body, you will be cleansing yourself inside and you will also feel it on the outside; and it is certain that your anxiety will begin to subside. Those are times of change and there is no better action than to look and feel better than ever, loving yourself will be your best medicine.

*Practicing any kind of sport heals the body and the mind, the sooner you put on your running shoes, and you will feel better.*

## 5.9 Know and recognize your best friend

If you have already begun to attack the symptoms of anxiety, I can assure you that you are already feeling the change; I can even imagine you smiling again and I am sure that you are starting to realize the benefits of having passed through this bad episode.

You find in yourself someone capable and stronger, someone who struggles and tries to get to know yourself, in order to make your life better. This feeling, of discovering that power that has always existed in you and notice the change, will be the best ally in your struggles.

Perhaps the main reason why anxiety came into your life was that you were pushing yourself aside. Improving your self-esteem is now a requirement, a need that you have to recover once you decide to take responsibility to enrich your life.

Maybe one of your biggest concerns, one of the reasons why the anxiety came into your life has been not being able to recognize what is your main goal in this life is. If that is so, I will try to help you.

You only have one main goal, trust me. Your main purpose is to take care of the most important person of your existence, that child who you once was and still lives in you; achieve to make yourself happy.

A direct action to help you reach your goal, is to look in your family photo albums or wherever you can find images of when you were a child, and a Once you have them, observe and try to remember who you were, what you felt, your dreams were, and thoughts were.

Remember what made you happy and as in those days your mission was quite simple, you wanted to enjoy your life as best as possible and remember that, almost always, you got it without effort.

It is time to appreciate yourself, it is time to treat yourself, and give yourself time to pamper yourself. Consider that in your reality you are the most important person. Talk with yourself, treat yourself well, do not punish or blame yourself, be aware of who you are.

With all this in mind, go back to the present and accept that your worries, anxieties and needlessness have kept you from your path. However, also observe how on this path, that you began to follow, that we are transiting together. You have returned to take responsibility for your happiness, the happiness of that child that you once were.

Now that you have recognized and remembered what the main purpose in your life is, in these moments when you face your problem struggling and taking responsibility, in these moments when you carry out actions aimed at reducing the symptoms of your anxiety, now that you are managing to create a better version of yourself, the time has come to recognize the change, it is time to accept and enjoy that new version that is being born in you.

Realizing who you are, acknowledge your conduct, your struggle and your change, will be the most powerful things you could do; a fact that should make you feel happy in any situation or instant, whether you live with anxiety or not; This power will be the force that will transform you into someone much more tenacious towards life, someone with more resources and abilities.

142

Working on yourself, you will realize the many benefits that this phase brings to your life. In the last chapter, I will confess many of what this struggle brought to mine life but, before coming to it and while you work to eliminate your anxiety, I hope that knowing some of the tricks that I used in my battle can help you, I have called them *"Tricks to utilize during your coexistence with anxiety."*

Be sure to still take action, keep changing, keep appreciating yourself, do not throw in the towel, because everything will surely change sooner than you thought possible.

Now that you feel and understand that the most important thing is you and you know that the way to staying on track is through your actions, review this chapter of actions as many times as you think it is necessary. The change must be real, the change must be yours.

*You are the most important person in your life, give yourself more of everything that brings you closer to life.*

# 6 Tricks to utilize during your coexistence with anxiety

*Act the way you want to feel.* Gretchen Rubin

*My life has been full of terrible misfortunes, most of which never happened.* Michel de Montaigne

In this chapter I try to remind you of some tricks I have used to fight and reduce the symptoms of anxiety

Living with this disorder is like living with their feelings and, there is nothing worse than to focus on how bad they make you feel, and making you feel powerless.

When you begin to notice that the symptoms increase, this is when we must put in place mechanisms that, as soon as possible, make us return to calmness; recognize them, associate them with our need for improvement and perform exercises to help you learn how to manage them once you have taken control and, once you are in control, you will have overcome the problem forever.

While giving meaning to my disorder, I understood that what we must regulate or choose to stop suffering from is fear. Anxiety does not determine who we are, it comes to teach us that we need a change, it is fear that is limiting us. Fear makes you feel small, incapable, sick, and different, without resources or feeling stuck. The worst thing is that if we do not face it, if we do not know how to treat it, it may be the one who controls us.

To control any fear, the symptoms must be our compass; the indicators of what we must change, fear or worry is not useful for anything other than that they increase. Therefore, recognizing and treating them when they show up, will be our priority.

To manage many of our symptoms and turn them from limitations into indicators, I used a trick; here I summarize some of them hoping that they can also help you to understand that you should be the one who has control over your life.

### Accept fear, and let it be. Make room for it

Most of the fears we have are not controllable on our part, we try to avoid them, but we still do not control them. Fear of dogs, spiders, betraying your partner, losing your job, fearing that your children use drugs, losing a family member ... *Have you thought about how much these fears depend on you?*

You can avoid walking in front of the houses that you know may have a dog, but you cannot avoid finding one when you turn the corner. Learn to live with them and as much as possible, recognize that if you learn to control yourself you can live without suffering for it.

### Say no to drugs or any unnatural substance

As I have mentioned throughout this book, drugs are one of the worst enemies in our lives, living with anxiety. Its effect is direct and immediate, just try a cup of coffee to find this out.

This trick is simple, avoid the exhilarating ones like coffee, red bull or Coca-Cola- (never stop having sex), and even more important, avoid any other type of drug that may affect your balance. Drugs such as hashish, speed, cocaine or the rest of the majority, rest assured, whether it is difficult for you to accept it or not, they will affect you to a great extent.

Maybe one of the main reasons why the anxiety came to your life lies in the use you made of these substances. Maybe in your case, like mine, the drugs do not go with your personality and the anxiety has come to your life for you to do understand it.

Whether you like it or not, if you want to eliminate the anxiety from your life, it is time to say no to drugs.

### *Do not focus on yourself and your feelings, divert your attention, use distractions*

As soon as you recognize that your symptoms are increasing, divert your attention. Stop appreciating what you feel and focus your mind on anything else you see, hear, feel or touch. Use your senses to focus on any element different from what you suffer.

You can use different techniques to distract your mind, like counting backwards from one hundred, review the capitals of countries you know, list soccer players and their positions or count the number of shoes you have in your closet.

I used the following technique when I felt that some sensation made the present difficult for me; As I walked through the streets, I looked at the license plates of the cars and began to make sums with the numbers until, without realizing it, the symptoms started depleting, and disappearing ..

It is good to recognize the symptoms when they show up, in order to understand the things that we must change. Once you have understood, it is necessary to carry out actions that make us feel at peace again. One action can be to look out and think about *what is happening around you?*

This trick is based on diverting attention to anything other than your symptoms. Using it, you will realize the direct relationship between thoughts and sensations. If you think of anxiety it will get bigger, but if on the other hand, you think of something else and you downplay what you feel, your symptoms will become smaller and smaller until they disappear.

### The anxiolytics, keep them close but not too close

The problem of feeling anxiety is in the lack of control we feel in different situations. So, a good tactic to regain that self-confidence, may be to take an anxiolytic tablet.

As I explained in previous chapters, try to be stronger and not depend on these medications, use them only if you do not find another possibility.

Especially at the beginning when the anxiety is stronger, take a pill with you, and it may help you feel more confident and, in the event that things get really bad (it only happens in your mind) these pills will help you feel better and will help you to sleep like an anesthetized bear; but, if you manage to be strong and not need them (which I know you can), you will realize that it is you who really has control.

### Learn and practice breathing techniques

We do not realize that the burden produced by anxiety directly affects our breathing, thereby directly increasing our tachycardia, the feeling of dizziness, sweating, and many of the symptoms that accompany this disorder.

If you start to feel dizzy or you lack air, when experiencing an anxiety crisis, you understand that there is nothing supernatural in it. You are provoking yourself without realizing that you are hyperventilating. The trick to stop doing this is to learn how to calm down.

It is likely that, in these conditions, trying to stay calm is not easy, so a good technique is to breathe in and in a plastic or paper bag. Thereby, increasing the levels of $CO_2$ needed in your blood that hyperventilation was reducing.

Learning to breathe deeper and slowly helps manage that impulsive acceleration which generates anxiety.

When you feel anxious, wherever you are and who you are with, prioritize yourself and breathe the best you can. You can use the trick, or technique of diverting attention and concentrate your thoughts on the breath. Relaxing will calm you down, restore you to a state of balance and help you recognize that control has always been within you.

### Observe yourself, recognize the present and learn to relativize

You are aware that your mind can lower your degree of anxiety but you are also aware that you can achieve the opposite.

I lived continuously worried, when at the beginning, I did not recognize the direct relationship between thoughts and symptoms. When I understood that I extended the symptoms in certain situations with my thoughts or lack of control, I began to observe myself until reaching the point that in certain situations, my priority was only one, calm my mind. I understood that I would not fall to the ground or suffer a heart attack or any other paranoia that at that moment I could imagine. I was learning to relativize.

Faced with those changes that you feel in your life, do not think about the way they limit you. When you live anxiously anticipating a catastrophic world around your fears, you think that something intense can always happen, and, this only increases your symptoms and the feeling of not being in control.

When I learned to observe myself and manage my symptoms, I generated an internal warning mechanism that told me:

It has arrived, *what are you doing? Are you letting yourself go again?* By recognizing and relativizing my symptoms or the importance of these, I quickly tried to return to calm down and, best of all, I accepted the reason and learned how to recognize the many things that I had yet to improve.

This mechanism would not only help me deal with anxiety but also with life in general, nerves, or any situation that could arise and I should learn to control.

*Do not worry about what people will say or think, and do not be catastrophic*

For example, when in social situations, vertigo makes you believe that you are going to fall to the ground, stop thinking about it, you will not fall and if you did, the blame was in thinking so much about it and the reaction you have provoked in yourself, not in your anxiety.

You can use any technique you know or simply learn to downplay the situation. Since I might happen to you, the vertigo appears in social situations, it understands that it is the burden of not feeling in balance and being surrounded by people which makes you feel that way, your lack of self-confidence; it is not anxiety, it is your mind. Understand that this concern is not real and that you are not dying, it also eliminates the shame you may feel because your life is much more important than what anyone else thinks of you.

Faced with the anguish that we generate in social situations, my tactic was simply to relax when I realized it; if, for example, during any activity I started to feel worse, I simply tried to relax internally without caring if the other person needed to hear something from me; the important thing was me, and maybe talking less could make me even more interesting and mysterious.

### Do not give too much importance to the place or situation

It is important that you do not get distracted in fleeing from the situation that caused the crisis. Overcome the problem in that moment, otherwise you may get used to relate that place or situation with fear, which could generate attacks in the future or condition you in certain situations

Everything begins in your head and we must focus on controlling the situations that change us. The circumstance or place does not matter, what matters is what we think about it.

### Learn how to meditate or try mindfulness

It might sound strange to you and I admit, that at the time, it seemed strange to me as well.

You may think that meditation is a crazy thing or a sectarian practice or you may already know the benefits it brings; Anyway, I encourage you to search the internet for the person who has been recognized (through scientific studies) as the happiest person in the world.

You will find the name, Mathieu Richard, a Buddhist monk who among other things as a good Buddhist does, meditates. If you continue reading about his philosophy of life you will see the direct relation that happiness and meditation have.

If you investigate something more about the benefits of meditation, you will observe that its main objective is to calm the mind and thoughts, that eternal inner turmoil that, especially living with anxiety, makes us feel insane. Meditation is based on breathing and relaxation, two main things that will help calm our symptoms. It seeks to help us learn how to observe what the reactions to our thoughts and symptoms are, and it helps us learn to recognize that what we feel was caused on our own, because of our way of thinking.

In the lotus position, levitating or walking, many of the actions we are taking to treat our anxiety are not very different from meditation.

*Try it!* Whether you are doing it right or wrong, it will bring you peace, improve your breathing and your heart rate and your anxiety will have decreased. With practice it will be easier to detect the causes that generate many of the symptoms that we are fighting.

### *Exercise*

Personally, exercising, or practicing a sport is the best and simplest of things that will help you reduce anxiety, and also, the fastest and most direct.

Exercising will eliminate negative thoughts and reduce many of your symptoms; you will calm your mind and improve your breathing and heart rate. Exercise is an all in one, you get to improve your life by doing simple activities.

It is also the simplest practice because you will not need to perform other activities such as diverting attention or controlling your mind, everything will come to place, and make sense when you exercise.

If you try it out, while you treat the anxiety you will notice its benefits instantly. After exercising, you will feel like your symptoms are decreasing. Do not leave for tomorrow a practice that you can start today.

### Eliminate negativity

Avoid negative thoughts, people, situations or places, avoid movies, books or negative news. Take anything depressing out of your life because it is time to believe in the world and in life, it is time to believe in ourselves.

Given the difficulty you feel accompanied by such complicated symptoms, any sign of denial can make you believe that it is better to throw in the towel, but that is the last thing you should do. Do not let your symptoms fool you, you are much stronger than your anxiety.

Negativity can make you believe that the world is the wrong place, that you are just a victim and that nothing depends on you, when the reality of life tells you and will always tell you, just the opposite.

Sooner or later, life shows you that you are responsible for what you feel, you are the only one able to get out of this or any problem that may arise. Believe in yourself, believe in your change; you are becoming someone more valuable, stronger and wiser, someone with more resources for life, in other words, a happier person.

Look for the positive and, if you do not see it, *fake it till you make it.* Many studies certify that we feel the same before a lived experience than an imagined one so, if the environment is not the most adequate, go out and look for a book, a movie or anything that can help you immerse yourself in another reality that fills you with motivation. This is the best time to dream, although we should do it while we are awake.

### Avoid monotony

Avoid laziness, laziness or the could not-care-less attitude. Sadness is the result of monotony and boredom and, as we saw before we defeat anxiety with positive energy.

Start doing different things, go to places you did not frequent, read books you did not read before, meet different people (meet people who have overcome a more serious problem than yours – it can help you relativize), sign up for a course or do other activities. Travel, laugh, eat, dream, sing, dance, love, try to perform activities that make you see life with new eyes because, whether you want it or not, you need a change of perspective.

If you still believe that every day is always the same, I encourage you to do a simple test; every morning when you wake up observe the sky and its clouds. Do you see any changes? I can assure you that there are no two days that are exactly the same.

Monotony, boredom, and even the sadness are only in your inside your head. So, it is time to change perspective.

### Learn how to say no

Anxiety is the result of anguish, of misunderstood burden, of unobserved suffering. When we feel anxious, our thoughts begin to attack us according to our symptoms. Our supposed terminal illness or our growing insanity, in the presence of such chaos, our brain does not stop overthinking about everything. There are so many thoughts and so none that make sense that we feel like we are going crazy to the point where we get dizzy and feel like we are falling to the ground.

We believe that thinking will bring us back to peace, but in reality it does the exact opposite.

Now is not the time to add burdens or any unnecessary tasks. Therefore, learn to say no to things you do not want to do or people who will not bring you peace, or positivity. Avoid all that unnecessary mental fuss.

Understand that this period of life is reserved for you. Now that you live with anxiety you are living a valuable time to be on your own and learn more about yourself. These are moments of self-love, days to soothe your mind and perform activities that bring you closer to life, to balance.

If there are things, circumstances or people that are going to keep you away from it all, learn how to avoid them.

If you need to give an explanation, you can use anxiety as an excuse or invent something that can best help you; you are the most important person in your life and now, you need love, especially self-love.

### Find praise from someone who loves you

The people who love you must be the mirror in which they reflect you, the embrace in which to comfort you.

Lean on those people who help you feel good, ate peace; those who do not demand anything from you, who understand and listen to you, those who are an extension of you, not the other way around.

Wrap yourself in smiles, a good atmosphere, good health and positivity, it is the best moment to feel modest, acknowledge it and, both with anxiety and without it, make this new lesson yours:

*Life is a long road in which we cannot travel alone. The better the company, and the more we learn with and from them, the nicer our journey will be.*

### Learn how to listen

Learning how to listen is perhaps one of the best activities to maintain a healthy social life. If, instigated by anxiety, we try to improve this task, we will not only improve our communication skills and we will make our friendships stronger, we will also be able to help ourselves from this activity to evade our symptoms and to know realities different from ours that can help us to relativize the importance we give to our problems.

If on social occasions your symptoms get worse, improve your breathing, try to calm down and focus on what they are saying, do not just hear, *Listen*!

As you are being more selective with your friends and the people who accompany you along the way, it is easy for the same social situations to change and you feel more comfortable and confident. So learn how to listen and give importance to those people you have chosen to keep by your side. Friendship is about giving, receiving and returning, a cycle that the better you run it, the more joy it will bring to your life.

Listening focuses on the present, it makes you a better friend, a better lover, a better brother; it improves your communication skills while helping you to evade the smallness of your world to understand that there is much more out there.

Since our main intention now is to give less value to our symptoms, if when you try to hold a conversation you put all your attention on what the other person is telling you, you will be focusing on other realities and discounting your symptoms.

There is more life, more realities, greater and different problems, we have to relativize while improving our environment and, listening, is a simple task that will bring us closer to change.

### Prepare yourself for the best

Just as we anticipate failure, we can also anticipate pleasure. The probability is the same because everything depends on where you put your attention and the opportunities you want to observe, believe and create.

There is a reality called "self-fulfilling prophecy" that says that people end up provoking what we anticipate; if you think about it, it is certain that in your life, as in that of any other there are many examples of this.

It is certain that if you expect good things you will tend to perceive and find the good. If on the contrary, you start the day thinking that you will have a bad time. You may even experience dizziness and really have a horrible day. You will be waiting for signs related to dizziness, or anything that can ruin your day.

For all this, *focus on the good*! Change that "*I already knew it* "mentality, for a: "*you see it is been great how I expected it, I made it possible*".

### Spend time with yourself and treat yourself

Whether things or people, moments or experiences, try treat yourself with things that make you feel more alive each day.

It is not necessary for them to be expensive, giving you more is about doing things for yourself, and things that make you gain hope.

You are changing, you are getting it and you deserve to be treated better than ever, you have to consider yourself as that great person that you have always been and that now with anxiety you know better.

Go for a walk, have that ice cream that you love, go on a trip, do an activity, read a book, ride a bicycle or go on an adventure, it is time for you to have fun. Feel the joy while you get to know yourself and improve. It is time that you spoil yourself, discover all of your potential and smile when you realize that you are lovingly taking care of that inner child that you once were, and is always by your side.

The time has come to remember and not forget that your main purpose in this life is one and very simple, to be happy.

With all these tips and the ones you will discover in your own way, the message becomes clearer, *you have become responsible for your life and you are working on it, you are a fighter and, being responsible for your life is the wisest action that you have been able to undertake now or never.*

Just as a sailor has to understand when to change course or how a compass works, many of these tricks can become tools that help you navigate the many different seas that you will have to navigate in this life.

*To control anxiety and any other fear, the symptoms are the indicators of what we should change. Recognizing them and treating them when they show up will be our best cure.*

# 7 My life after anxiety

*Be water my friend.* Bruce Lee

In these pages I have tried to tell a story, an experience that became a path from which I learned a great lesson, while learning to live with a strange disease apparently meaningless and unknown, called anxiety.

In that stage of my life in which fear took hold of me and I felt crazy thinking that my life had changed forever, and worry filled my days.

After complicated beginnings in which it was difficult for me to accept what was happening to me and I could not understand the reason for those insufferable symptoms, there came a day I decided to help myself, and looked for help. Without knowing it, I had made the best decision.

A psychologist, a few sessions and a book, would help change the way in which I confront that then complicated present. This change would take the form of a new path that would help me overcome anxiety for the rest of my life.

Overcoming that challenge that life put before me would make me internalize tools that would help me manage problems better, while understanding the meaning and way of dealing with anxiety. The intention of this book has been to help you understand this process, a lesson that if I had known it when this problem arose in my life, it would have helped me to overcome it much more easily and quickly.

Basically these would be my steps:

- Recognize that those complicated symptoms had a single diagnosis: anxiety.

I was not going crazy or suffering from cancer or suffering from a heart condition; there was no other disease in the world that encompassed so many different symptoms, there were no other options.

Accepting it and recognizing that it was really what I was facing, gives you much more peace than you can imagine, while it helps you eliminate many worries and direct you towards a specific goal. Knowing the problem allows you to approach your solution.

- Trying to discover what my causes were, recognizing those errors that had caused me to discover words like the homeostasis or the reptilian brain.

After knowing my motives, everything made sense. Facing them would be the solution to the problem and the only way to overcome anxiety. Recognizing my symptoms, when and why these occurred, would be the compass that indicated the path towards my goal.

- Taking responsibility and working on myself. Life does not change if you do not change, it is a fact; the world is not good or bad, but as you want to perceive it. Only you can change your reality and there is only one possible way, take action.

Against anxiety, as with any other difficulty in life, the only way to avoid a wild goose chase is to face it by recognizing that it is you and not the world who will overcome the problem. Waiting, avoiding or believing in magic potions will not do you any good. As soon as you decide and use that strength that you carry inside everything, even the power of your symptoms, will begin to change.

- Motivating myself, taking action. If there were things that I did not like, only I could fight them, I had to invest my time in the most important person in my life, myself.

I would put to use as many of the tips and tricks I mentioned in the previous chapter, and I would discover how the symptoms and my causes were related.

With taking action, I would discover one of the most important secrets of anxiety, I could calm my mind to eliminate my symptoms. It was I who had the control. To discover this fact and to put myself to the test would only confirm that what I suffered had a name and that with my actions, I could overcome it.

- The last step is to remember and internalize the lesson learned. Know that you have new tools and that you are stronger. Having been able to overcome this difficult stage, it is useful to deal with other future problems that may arise in life.

I knew that anxiety would never control my life as I learned to overcome it and I would know how to do it again. Remember the process and use your own tools, leave an imprint in your brain that assures you that no disease can condition you, you know that you always were, are and will be stronger.

Anxiety made me wiser, made it made me realize that inner potency that we carry inside, a force capable of achieving the greatest of feats if you really decide to believe in you, made me understand that power without control is useless and that, it is our responsibility to take control of our lives.

Those lessons would bring new rewards to my life, some would be temporary but others, will always be a part of me.

## 7.1 The benefits of anxiety

*Happiness is beneficial for the body, but grief develops the powers of the mind.* Marcel Proust

*What does not kill me, makes me stronger.* Friedrich Nietzsche

As I told you before, you are now aware that you can turn anxiety into an enemy that will persecute you if you want, for the rest of your days or, you can be more intelligent and make it your ally, understanding it, knowing that it carries a message and struggling to decipher that truth will help you improve your quality of life.

If you adopt smart solutions you will realize that the effects of your change are quick and direct. You will feel better in a few days and best of all, you will embrace new attitudes in the form of tools that will help you develop in life.

If you still do not have them (solutions) all with you, I encourage you to try and start without waiting for tomorrow; there is nothing more important in your life than your own happiness and it is impossible to be happy if you are not functioning properly within.

On this path back to life, you will begin to feel many of the benefits of having gone through this tough stage. If you have started working on it, you probably have already noticed.

You must accept that anxiety has come to you with a message and working on yourself helps make the journey fun as well as beneficial. You will slowly understand that your life is better and you know yourself better, you will understand that you have a more important meaning to life, to your people, to your actions and, assisted by this lesson, you will smile again, maybe more and better than you did before.

Coping with anxiety brings you closer to your path, it will make you realize of your responsibility to life.

Everything depends on the way you look at things, so the best way to perceive this stage is to realize the need to bring to light that fighter you have inside you and, of all the benefits that you have lived with this problem can bring to your life, improving many aspects that anxiety has shown us we needed to change. Make this saying your mantra: "every cloud has a silver lining".

Among the many assets that anxiety will bring to your life, I am going to tell you some of the ones it brought to mine:

- I understood that I am responsible for what happens to me and that only I can change my reality. In any situation experienced, the sooner you stop feeling like a victim, you will begin to see the light, leaving the problem and approaching the solution.

Living, learning and taking action, made me feel content and, that feeling, would become a part of me forever. Internalize this message, that truth together with the memory of having been able to do something as complicated, destabilizing, mysterious, seemingly, and meaningless as anxiety, helped me overcome many of my future fears, recognizing that many of them were created by me and my thoughts.

I knew that before any problem could arise in the future, the process would be similar to the one I used to overcome anxiety.

With your change, with your action, you can identify the progress and the message. Be aware of the direct relationship between action and results. By taking action, you will recover your hopes, the true motor of life that will make you understand that overcoming this and any problem is and always will be possible.

- I understood causality. That which comes to our life is an effect fruit of one or several actions of the past. I can apply this idea to any event to realize that throwing balls out does nothing but lengthen the anguish; in this way, in the face of any problem, I look first to what my causes may be to evaluate how to reverse the situation.

- I eliminated the hypochondria of my life by understanding that the carelessness did nothing but make my condition worse. Focusing on my symptoms associating them with other diseases was the worst of the actions to eliminate them.

- I learned to relativize life and my problems by understanding that adding fuel to the fire only increased the burns.

While relativizing, I found some peace to discover that anxiety is a lesser evil that can be treated and that, living with it could perhaps help me improve many other facets of my life that could and should be improved.

- I understood that the drugs did not suit me well, realizing that, and the mere fact of fooling around with them, increased many of my unpleasant symptoms.

This lesson is a part of me, and as of today I choose to stay away from what I know affects me and hurts me. I discovered that we are chemistry and putting certain substances without meaning, knowledge or need in my body could produce temporary or life-long reactions.

- Using several of the tricks I indicated in the "Tricks to utilize during your coexistence with anxiety" chapter, I learned techniques that would become tools that help me calm down or change perspective when necessary.

- I understood the effect of thoughts in my life and created a mechanism to identify and eliminate negative thoughts when they came to my mind. Realities such as the water experiment supported this need.

If we do not realize it, we will see the world in the way they taught us or we will feel like victims of a reality that we cannot change. If instead we decide to take responsibility, we will realize that it is possible to see the world in a much more intelligent and healthy way, one that helps us modify our reality, by orienting it towards our dreams.

- With the practice of sports or doing a physical activity, and a change in my diet I improved physically and psychologically, bringing benefits and pleasant experiences. I made changes in my life that became part of the new version of myself, and to this day keep with me.

- I learned to have more willpower. Things such as going for a run when I did not feel like it, and later noticing its benefits, taking responsibility for my problems, solving and facing realities such as anxiety and fear, have left their mark on me. I know that within me I have the strength and the necessary tools to overcome any challenge; if apathy or discouragement becomes strong, I remember that I am a fighter and that it is not the problems that make you feel bad but the way you see them and react to them.

- I improved my social circles by moving away from places, people or situations that made me feel worse. My whole world would change by guiding my actions and enjoying more of what made me feel better and more alive.

- I understood that in life we must recognize who the important people are and why. After experiencing that period of my life, my relationships and friendships are much healthier, stronger and long lasting.

Friendship has acquired a different value, to love yourself is also knowing how to surround yourself with people who appreciate you. Life is about giving, receiving and returning, and to enjoy this cycle as best as possible, there is nothing better than to surround yourself with family and good friends.

- I learned to do more activities that made me feel better both inside and out. Things that brought me closer to balance, traveling, reading, doing activities of adventure, going to the movies or the theater, sports and many other tasks, which became my best gifts, that make me feel content and live.

- Accompanied by anxiety, before my discoveries and actions, I began to feel the changes, surpassing it I understood that the majority of mental or physical problems that can come to our life, have a cause and a message, and that, avoiding or fearing them can bring even greater problems.

*The basis of all change is to understand the causes and act accordingly,* this is a truth that could be used before any problem that may arise.

- Knowing the above, I would embark on adventures that before having lived with anxiety I would not have believed possible.

Facing and overcoming this problem would make me understand that the force we carry within us, a power that we can use whenever we need to, is an engine that we must use to pursue many of our dreams.

- I overcame many of my fears realizing that, faced with the barrier, we must stop and think whether it is necessary to continue like this or face it. Understanding the reason for your reactions to your fears helps you to give real value to things, to guide you and, if necessary, to change course.

- I learned how to live in the present and to enjoy the little things in life. Using several tricks during my coexistence with anxiety, I learned to focus on the now, while looking to stop feeling those symptoms, while giving me experiences and moments that brought me closer to life,

These small periods of life in which I managed to stop feeling anxiety, led me to the only reality that exists, the present.

- I also started to give less importance to what people thought or said. If before a group of people I began to feel instability and / or feel dizzy, I stopped giving importance to what they could think of me and simply calmed down.

- I learned to control my impulsiveness, thoughts and emotions. From the imbalance I soon went to a balance greater than I had ever felt before, I was learning to value things in their proper measure, facing them for what they really were.

-I learned to know myself better both physically and mentally. I recognized my causes, the messages, my reactions and I struggled to change what that reptilian brain had asked me to change.

- I realized that anxiety is fueled by fear, that symptoms depend on the thoughts (of the fear we feel at the imbalance) and that there are actions that can attack those symptoms. Internalizing my actions I overcame many fears and faced new ones.

All these are just some of the benefits that can come with understanding anxiety, destroying its message and acting accordingly.

The disorder itself is not bad, its alarming symptoms leave no room for options other than fighting to regain control of our lives, and this struggle, this personal duel of self-improvement, brings a great lesson in your for life.

In my case, fighting the problem made me discover the formula to overcoming any future grief that could arise. Whether I realized at that time or not, this lesson, made me become a much stronger and confident person.

I know that you, just like me, have decided to fight this. Speaking as a former anxious person, I can assure you that the anxiety is not stronger than you and that it will never control your life if you want.

If you choose to act and take responsibility, you will discover that once you overcome this challenge, you will have become a person who is valued and respected, someone with more resources and capabilities. Before any factor, illness or situation that you need to face, making use of this lesson will be the best of your actions.

With each new step you will realize that you are living better, you know yourself more, and you give more meaning to your life, your people and your actions. You are responsible for your life, you improve your reality.

## 7.2 I am and will be the strongest

*It always seems impossible until it is done.* Nelson Mandela

*I learned that courage was not the absence of fear, but the triumph over it. The brave man is not he who does not feel afraid, but he who conquers that fear.* Nelson Mandela

You will have noticed that the two quotes in which the chapter begins are both from Nelson Mandela, one of the best examples to help you understand what I mean, when I speak of the inner strength that every human being carries within.

Mandela was a person of flesh and blood, what differentiated him from most other people was his inner strength, his courage; an energy capable of making him believe in his dreams before a reality in which any other human being would have chosen to collapse completely.

Given the total safety of finishing his days in a one by two meters wide jail cell, having been sentenced to life imprisonment, he decided to believe in another reality, clinging to an idea that would keep him healthy and sane, the idea that one day he would be free and would also free his people. Maybe he was the only person in the world to believe in this possibility, but Mandela acted day after day as if that were the way to turn that impossible into reality.

Believe it or not both you and Mandela are made of the same substance, you can both choose, you can also decide to believe in yourself and let your inner strength sprout. It will help you obtain the greatest of victories even when nobody believes it possible.

Before all of your problems, repeat this phrase several times "all bad things have a good side", it will help you to know how to lead, coexist and overcome any complicated moment that may come up in your life.

In the face of anxiety, we can help ourselves and realize that the actions we are forced to carry out in order to return to balance will really make us feel the benefits; We can see it as an evil that, if you choose to fight and improve your life, will bring many good things.

Once you begin to take action of the problem, you will realize that you feel even better than before having known and lived with anxiety, not only have you won or are you struggling to overcome a great difficulty in your life but, more importantly, you are surpassing yourself.

While taking action you will realize that attacking the problem and overcoming it, is a necessary obligation that will bring you closer to a happier life.

If you have followed the process, you have understood and given a name to your symptoms, you are getting to know yourself better to understand your causes and you are carrying out actions that bring you back to peace. You will be overcoming the fear of anxiety and, once its overcome, it will be completely indifferent, and it may or may not appear again in your life. You will have made yours a method to understand it and value it for what it is and you will know that, if it reappears, you will face it and overcome it without having to suffer for it.

Living the process that I explain in this book brought an important lesson and it was from that experience when I recognized that the disease, initially so inexplicable, worrying and almost mystical, was something simple, logical, biological and easy to solve.

I discovered that there were one or several causes and a process with which to deal with both, and future anxieties or blocking fears that could arise in my life. As if it were a common cold, I realized that there was an antidote, I had found a formula to overcome anxiety forever.

As I was saying, different forms of this disorder came back to my life, but it would never be the same. As soon as it showed up, I automatically recognized the symptoms, I looked for what my reasons were, I discovered its new message, carrying out the tips and tricks that you learned, made the symptoms disappear and made those changes that my life needed.

Thanks to having understood this reality, the future anxieties had their last days coming and, their symptoms would no longer be able to destabilize me at all. It was only during that first anxiety attack in which ignorance, fear and worry, only made my symptoms and many of my days worse. After that process, understanding what anxiety is and why it comes to your life, giving it the right value makes it almost automatically disappear.

Having internalized many of these actions, recognizing it for what it is and not giving it more value, accepting that it brings a message about what that unknown intelligence called the reptilian brain wanted for my life, made everything much easier.

I have repeated many concepts throughout this book with an intent, to help you internalize and make these ideas yours; once you recognize this message as yours, you will stop fearing anxiety forever.

If this problem comes back to your life, as it happened to me, it will never be the same, it will not condition you or make you feel unstable, or even your symptoms will be as aggressive as they had been before, and treating it will not need so much time or effort on your part.

It is easy to understand why it will come easy to face anxiety, if it decides to show up again:

- First of all, you will recognize the problem for what it really is. It may come in the form of tremors, dizziness or cold sweats or all of the above; the form does not matter.

Giving it the right value appraisal will cause the potency of its symptoms to decrease to a great extent so that it does not limit or control your day to day.

- You will immediately know that it carries a message and that you are responsible for discovering it. You will study your life, your changes and you will realize what may be affecting you. Maybe you are just experiencing a somewhat stressful period and your life habits have worsened, whatever it may be, once you modify the mistakes or wrong actions, the anxiety and your symptoms will begin to wane.

- You will have internalized tools to combat and solve many of your problems, you will know that it is possible and even pleasant to get going and, you will go into action automatically, without giving a lot of thought to the issue or feel powerless.

- You may find yourself much better physically, and with more energy than ever, so you will face your problems in a more responsible, active and positive way

In my case, exercise has formed a part of my life since anxiety made me understand its importance and benefits, the strength of will acquired with it helps me to face challenges or needs of life without leaning on excuses that can block me.

- Emotionally you will have known how to surround yourself with better people, you will have understood the importance of your thoughts in your life, you will move in better environments and you will even recognize that some drugs have a direct effect on your organism. If, on the other hand, you have not followed these tips, you may observe that among your possible causes these are and, as it happened to me, you may accept that, for example, drugs do not go with you.

- Rationally you will know the many of the tricks that helped you overcome that first time and you will start using them without realizing it, automatically

- You know that in the past you fought, you won and you became stronger. This message will be part of your life and whether you want it or not, either in the face of anxiety or any other difficulty, your brain will use this lesson to draw back that inner strength that you always (although sometimes you do not realize or you do not want to believe it) have taken with you.

Before any type of grief that life puts before you, identify that in the past you overcame it, and will always be your best ally.

In my case, if I feel that anxiety has returned to my life, my actions are quick, simple and direct:

- I observe that I feel some anxiety, some symptom makes me realize it, and I know it is nothing different because I know how it shows up. I look for information in my memory and I recognize that I know how to face the problem, moreover, the memory tells me that It is not a problem but an opportunity and I know that, just as I overcame it that first time, I will do it again sooner and without the need to suffer for it.

- I eliminate any type of stimulating substance such as coffee or Cola-Cola, to reduce some of the direct symptoms. Recovering some peace is the basis for returning to equilibrium, and any artificial stimulant would have the opposite effect to what I need at this moment.

- I relativize the symptoms and I realize that I am not going to die, moreover, I am not even going to faint. I know that tachycardia is normal and that the less I think about it, the sooner it will disappear and I will stop feeling it. I understand that sweat, dizziness and other sensations depend directly on my breathing and my thoughts. I also identify that the worst action is to focus on them or worry, and the sooner I divert my attention, the sooner they will diminish and disappear.

These symptoms should only serve as a compass to know what I should change or improve in my life. Focusing on what it is making me feel or distress me in excess, is what is keeping me in that worrying state. I know that I am responsible for improving my present, which is the way, before the face of worry.

My thoughts focus on relativizing its power and use many of my tricks and tips to soften their symptoms while I make the changes that they are telling me. It is time to take care of yourself.

- I learned to manage social settings. I know that the thoughts of others should not affect me, and that certain symptoms are provoked in these circumstances and that social phobia does not make any sense.

Knowing that I am not crazy and that I am stronger than my problem, this social concern coupled with anxiety does not usually last beyond recognizing its relationship with my first feeling of vertigo. I take a deep breath, I know that the message that anxiety brings will help me to feel better and with or without anxiety I go forward, and try not to avoid this type of situations.

- I observe myself and look for new causes within me. Perhaps I returned to environments that have nothing to do with me, the work I do or the way I look at it is stressing me out. I have returned to a sedentary life or, simply, I have given too much value to a thing or a person and I feel like the world is falling on me. There are millions of reasons; so, it is necessary to look within us to see which our reasons are, and the best way to understand the changes that anxiety wants in your life is to observe when and why your symptoms are presented.

- I admit to the actions that I took in their day and I choose those that I consider appropriate before the new causes that anxiety brings. I know I was able to overcome it and I will do it again, I accept that all bad things has its good side, and I smile as I face this new challenge.

Following these steps, in a few days, I felt better than before this new warning was presented.

The anxiety comes to tell me that a new virus is entering my life, once I recognize it and eliminate it, I will live in harmony again with what life, my essence or whatever you prefer to call it, considers best for me. The moment you accept what the message is, you will manage to overcome it forever.

Knowing that inner strength and bringing it out to combat the grief that life puts before you, serves to show you that you are also, were and always will be stronger than you think. The courage has always been inside you and, it is at times like this, when you have to utilize it more than ever.

## 7.3 You put the limits

*Argue your limitations and sure enough, they are yours.* Richard Bach

*Never say never, because limits, like fears are often justa n ilusion.* Michael Jordan

That path that I relate to in this book, is a period that began at the moment when anxiety came to my life and would end when I managed to make it disappear completely. Now I remember it as one of the best stages of my life.

Understanding the reality of my problem and working to overcome it, I managed to become someone stronger, more stable, more confident and more proactive; I realiized that the path and the effort was made once I had decided to take responsibility, and not act as a victim of that reality that was in my life. I learned to discover what my true potential was.

That battle helped me believe in me more, and set bigger goals, much more than I would have thought possible before suffering that initially complicated and unknown anxiety.

That illness that at first made me believe that fear would control the rest of my days, had achieved the opposite. To become more self-confident, a person willing to fight for their dreams with or without fears, someone that had discovered that they had the tools within and that would help live a fuller life.

Anxiety made me understand that fear is as strong or as small as we decide to make it. We can choose to be the ones who take control of our lives, or do the opposite. The fear that blocks us is only in your head and, if you want, you can make it disappear.

If, in the face of a fear, we are stuck, we remain terrified before their symptoms and we do not go any further. The feeling of dread will control our present. If we do the opposite and recognize that in fear there is a relationship between thought and feeling, we will understand that there are actions to calm the symptoms down, and we can act improving the thought that caused that fear; we will have managed to find the formula to direct our own life, whether fear is present or not.

If for example I feel dizziness or tachycardia (symptoms) before a certain situation, (reaction provoked by the thought associated with the circumstance) and I decide to act on it by recognizing the reason for what I feel; I have the power to choose to relativize the problem (change the thought) and find a way (for example, breathe more deeply and slowly) that brings me back at peace. I will have managed to control my reaction and master the symptoms and my anxiety.

If I observe the cause of my change and then act and alter my reaction to it, I will be responsible for what I feel, and not fear. I will take control, and anxiety will not have the power to control me.

Observing examples like this one, you realize that in life you can live, do or feel what you choose; you are the one who is putting limits, if you choose to.

After taking responsibility, facing and overcoming anxiety, a new and better version of myself was born.

That stronger new me, recognized that many of the limitations that I decided to believe, had to disappear. I knew that the responsibility was mine alone. I could make it possible and, overcome that problem, I had already proven it to myself.

That new me, in many unrecognizable aspects was more extroverted, self-sufficient and independent, more responsible and less fearful, recognizing that we are not only responsible for our lives but also creators of our realities.

Like a caterpillar in its transformation stage suffers the insufferable, to get out of the cocoon to become a butterfly, those difficult times had given me not only learning and knowledge but also wings in the form of new attitudes or automatic responses that I could use before problems that could present themselves in life. I had learned that we should not stop before the fear that blocks us, but try to face it by learning from it and from ourselves.

Growing up in the face of adversity that would be the best medicine against anxiety and any problem or duel that could arise. That new self with wings was preparing to live adventures that in those times many people (starting with myself) would have considered impossible, even more having recently lived a hard, lasting and totally destabilizing anxiety.

These were some of the new experiences that I would embark on after overcoming that problem:

A few months after getting over it, I got a job in a city that made me daydream, the one where all roads lead to, Rome. I did not think it was possible to fall in love with a place, but that is how it was. I arrived with a four-month contract to end up living there (I made it possible) for more than 9 years.

- I would learn a language that excited me while I knew people from different parts of the world; couples, friends or extraordinary friends who would become part of what I consider my people today.

- I would work in one of the oldest universities in the world, La Sapienza in Rome for several years.

- I would travel alone to Southeast Asia for a few months facing new challenges such as doing it alone or leaving work in times of crisis.

- I would create a company with several friends and I would be able to sell products in such exclusive places such as the Trevi Fountain or the Vatican.

- I would move to work as a director in a small startup on the other side of the pond, in Mexico, another place that fascinated me because of its history and culture.

- I would go paragliding, I would try the fly board, zip line, surf and a host of activities that attracted me and at that time I did not know.

- I would do part of the road to Santiago also alone. Facing an experience that, knowing me, I did not think possible.

- I would go live on an island and get the title of skipper to escape to new adventures when the occasion arose.

- I would write this book and...

- I would continue believing in myself to continue making some of my dreams come true, helping me with the courage that gives us to recognize that many of our fears (as would happen with anxiety) had their days numbered.

Recognizing that these fears would never condition my life but, on the contrary, it would impel me to try and make new experiences come true that, although fear tried to intimidate me, I wanted and needed to live.

I know that there are countless people with lives more successful or extraordinary than mine but, I recognize that this new me would make many dreams and experiences come true that before having embarked on the path I have described in this book, I would not have believed possible.

I was always aware that the dreaded anxiety could return, but I had learned that it would never have the power to control my life.

As in the existence of any person, many problems would come but, that great lesson, would help me to take action to go in search of what was worth living.

In the same way that it happened to me, your anxiety came to tell you that you lived things that did not go with you and thanks to their insufferable symptoms did not leave you more options than to face it, that is why as soon as you act on it, it will still let you enjoy life even while you live with your symptoms.

You will become aware of your power, your life is changing and you know that you make it possible; recognizing this you will notice that every day that passes by, you feel happier.

Once you have returned to a balanced life, you will have become someone better, a stronger person with more self-love, someone capable of facing many of their fears and one who knows how to choose what they want or not in their life, you will have learned that nobody but yourself can control your life.

Your new version will have internalized mechanisms that will help you to face new challenges, actions that maybe before knowing anxiety, you did not think were possible either.

Experience teaches you that it is possible that in the future, anxiety will reappear, action shows you that there really is nothing to worry about. For all this, if one day the anxiety comes back to your life, simply smile. You have learned the lesson, and soon you will realize that there is nothing to fear but much to learn. Your new self will recognize and relativize the symptoms, you will have a new attitude and automatically act by attacking the problem. Listening to your anxiety you will make you realize that *for every bad there is good*.

You will have learned that anxiety comes into our lives with a purpose. Although we cannot understand with our rational brain, it tries to make us understand that we need a change. Maybe before destabilizing our lives we tried to communicate, maybe that day we felt an unusual headache or an uncontrollable desire to cry, was nothing other than it asking us for a change.

Our desire to demonstrate, to direct our lives using other people's compass, our rush to return to peace or divert attention with alcohol, drugs or television to postpone the change, do nothing but light that wick that one day it exploded giving us something much stronger; Anxiety came into our lives to stay.

Before the unknown, before such a big change, we initially fear for our life and our sanity, hypochondria takes over us making us fear the worst, we feel that the end is near but, the days go by and whether we want to believe it or not, we are still standing .

Time passes by, but the symptoms do not and that is when we must realize the reality, what we suffer has no other name, it is only anxiety and its intention is far from ending our lives, it has come so that we learn from it improving our quality of life, it is our sole purpose.

This is the message I was deciphering while trying to return to reach balance: the sooner you accept it and work on your change, all of those symptoms that you are suffering will disappear, and you will recover your life.

With taking action, you will realize that a new version of yourself is born, you are becoming someone with more resources before life.

Once the lesson has been overcome and understood, you will become much stronger and will be able to face many of those fears that, before knowing the anxiety, had conditioned your life and surely avoided it; You will have managed to get out of the labyrinth in which your old self had you locked up giving life to someone more responsible and efficient, a new you with wings that will allow you to go much further than you thought possible, you will have learned to overcome any fear that tries to condition your life, forever.

I know that you already feel the change, you are taking responsibility and you notice how anxiety is not and never was stronger than you; You know that with, both facing this problem and any challenge that life puts before you, *limits are set by you.*

## 7.4 Everything you needed has always been within you

*And God, here you were inside me, and outside I was looking for you.* Reflections of Saint Agustíne

I am not a fan of coincidences and the simple fact that you are here, more specifically reading this book, helps me support this theory.

Birth is a miracle in which a single sperm wins a race against millions of opponents and if we add to this victory those of our ancestors and the different circumstances that had to occur to make them known, liked and procreated, it is easy to understand that whether we want to believe it or not, we are a true miracle of nature.

The probability that you and I are alive is close to absolute zero and, if we add to this miracle the fact that you are reading this book today, it is difficult to believe that everything is a mere coincidence.

Maybe the reason why this book came into your hands is the same for which months ago I myself decided to work on giving birth to this new reality in the form of a book, help you make the leap, understand that overcoming anxiety is not only possible but also much simpler and necessary than you could believe. The only thing you needed was always with you, that inner strength that I hope I helped you recover.

Undertaking the path that I tell in this book, taking responsibility for my life, researching, improving myself and doing all the actions to overcome the problem, would not have been possible without using that power that we have inside, that force capable of surprising you and creating new and incredible realities, like this book.

Realizing and recognizing that everything we need to face any duel we carry inside, is the best engine to make any of your dreams come true.

Many centuries ago, a saint and philosopher gave a good faith of what I mean, his name was St. Augustine and in one of his phrases he recognized this great truth, *"So many years of trying to find God outside, finally made me realize that he was always inside me"*.

We have reach the end of this road, in with which I hope I have helped you bring to light that inner strength that you have always carried with you; I know that if you have taken action, or are doing it now, you yourself had shown it to yourself.

This is the end of a road but many others will soon begin. So, I would love to say goodbye helping you to understand and discover which may be yours.

Try to visualize a long and tortuous path that you are slowly leaving behind...

You can see its end and noticing it, you smile. You smile because you realize that you were able to overcome it and, while you laugh and recognize it, you keep walking.

You feel lighter and happier, more confident and freer than you have ever felt before. You know there are only a few steps left, you can see the end...

Close to that finish line, you see an object, an indication, a signal, you will soon discover what it is trying to reveal, you have only a few steps left, the sign is getting closer and closer.

You feel immensely happy to recognize that you have managed to finish one of the hardest stages of your life, you know that you have learned a lot from this path and from yourself. From now on you depend on yourself, and it has become clear to you that the responsibility is and will always be yours.

You feel the taste of victory, you have achieved it and this will be the best of your lessons, accompanied by this sensation that you approach the signal with, and observe what it indicates...

It is a large sign that points to a mile, mile zero, a place where the old dies and the new is born, the starting point of all roads, the beginning of your infinite possibilities.

Surprisingly, you discover how countless doors open before you...

The options are endless and that is why you notice how doubts assail you, it is hard for you to decide which path to follow, but just at the beginning of each of them you notice some words, a lesson that you will burn in your memory, a phrase that reminds you of how you were able to overcome this hard challenge that life put before you and now you leave behind.

A caption that reads:

*You can make it possible*

# A note to the reader

The main objective that I have pursued with this book has been to help other people to understand and give meaning to what they suffer, trying to show them that sometimes the only thing that is needed is and has always been within ourselves.

I have focused on the message of anxiety, because this was the challenge that life put before me, making me observe this great truth. But I also believe that, by following this path we can overcome any fear or block, any problem that is taking us away from the life we really deserve but do not enjoy, due to leaving ourselves aside.

Knowing that if *The End of Anxiety* had existed in my past, it would have helped me a lot to face that problem that I suffered, I would like to ask you a favor:

If you have enjoyed this book, understood it and made the message yours; as long as you consider that it has been able to help you improve your life and believe that you can also help other people, I would like you to help me spread the message.

If you know someone who is going through a bad period of their life, which you think may need a change of perspective whatever the reason may be. If you know someone who complains about the world but has ceased to take responsibility. If you know someone who has diseases like stress, anguish or anxiety, or if you just liked the book and you think it might be interesting to share it with other people, I would love for you to help others to learn about it too.

You can do it by lending it to them, bringing it up in conversation, or simply suggesting it to them; you can give it away or help more people know about it by making a good review on the sales websites or on social networks. There can be many ways that can mean a new beginning in the existence of so many people, helping them to remember that there is a better world for themselves if they decide to take responsibility.

Also, *The End of Anxiety* collaborates directly with the nonprofit organization, *Vicente Ferrer*; an organization that I was able to see in person during one of my trips to India, a place where I can assure work constantly by coming up with solutions to solve dramatic realities such as poverty, malnutrition, abuse or social inequality. With all this, understand that an action as simple as a good criticism, not only helps that this message can improve the lives of many people, but also that they are directly collaborating in making this a better world.

As I hope you have understood, this is a book about taking action and one that you can do right now, at no cost to you but with a direct impact on the world, is to share this experience with the rest of the people, an action that will surely bring many good things to your life.

### Help to make this message reach more people

- Give this book as a gift to someone you feel may need it

- Take a picture with the book and publish it by tagging the book on Facebook or other social media, or become a fan of the page.

- If this book has helped you, help others discover what it can also bring to them by describing your experience on the Amazon page.

Printed in Great Britain
by Amazon